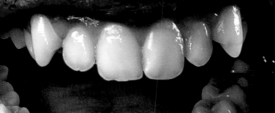

CANNIBAL SERIAL KILLERS

Nicki Peter Petrikowski

The Psychology of Serial Killers

Enslow Publishing
101 W. 23rd Street
Suite 240
New York, NY 10011
USA
enslow.com

Published in 2016 by Enslow Publishing, LLC.
101 W. 23rd Street, Suite 240, New York, NY 10011

Library of Congress Cataloging-in-Publication Data
Names: Petrikowski, Nicki Peter, author.
Title: Cannibal serial killers / Nicki Peter Petrikowski.
Description: New York, NY : Enslow Publishing, [2016] | Series: The
  psychology of serial killers | Includes bibliographical references and index.
Identifiers: LCCN 2015031488 | ISBN 9780766072824
Subjects: LCSH: Serial murderers—Juvenile literature. | Cannibalism—Juvenile literature. |
Criminal psychology—Juvenile literature.
Classification: LCC HV6515 .P475 2016 | DDC 364.152/32--dc23
LC record available at http://lccn.loc.gov/2015031488

Printed in the United States of America

To Our Readers: We have done our best to make sure all websites in this book were active and appropriate when we went to press. However, the author and the publisher have no control over and assume no liability for the material available on those websites or on any websites they may link to. Any comments or suggestions can be sent by e-mail to customerservice@enslow.com.

Photo Credits: Cover, p. 1 Dundanim/Shutterstock.com (mouth); throughout book chrupka/Shutterstock.com (black background), Merkushev Vasiliy/Shutterstock.com (red background), Tiberiu Stan/Shutterstock.com (brain waves activity); p. 4 © Orion Pictures Corporation/Courtesy: Everett Collection; p. 9 Millard H Sharp/Science Source/Getty Images; pp. 11, 13 © North Wind Picture Archives; p. 16 Private Collection/Mithra-Index/Bridgeman Images; p. 18 Linda Davidson/The Washington Post via Getty Images; p. 20 Prisma/UIG/Getty Images; p. 22 Enslow Publishing; p. 24 Arapahoe County Sheriff's Office via Getty Images; p. 26 Florida DOC/Getty Images News/Getty Images; p. 28 © Everett Collection; pp. 30, 78, 82, 86, 96, 111, 118, 128 © AP Images; p. 32 Zdravinjo/Shutterstock.com; p. 34 Hulton Archive/Getty Images; p. 38 Apic/Hulton Fine Art Collection/Getty Images; p. 42 Magnus Manske/Wikimedia Commons/Karl Denke/public domain; p. 44 Olga Meffista/Shutterstock.com; p. 47 Wikimedia Commons/Enriqueta Martí/public domain; p. 48 Public Domain; p. 51 Ossie LeViness/NY Daily News Archive via Getty Images; p. 54 NY Daily News Archive via Getty Images; p. 56 Public Domain; pp. 59, 64 ullstein bild via Getty Images; p. 61 Tim Schredder/Wikimedia Commons/Hannover cemetery stoecken grave Fritz Haarmann victims.jpg/CC BY-SA 2.0 de p. 68 Imagno/Hulton Archive/Getty Images; p. 70 © Daily Mail/Rex/Alamy; p. 73 Francis Miller/The LIFE Picture Collection/Getty Images; p. 75 Frank Scherschel/The LIFE Picture Collection/Getty Images; p. 88 Terry Smith/The LIFE Images Collection/Getty Images; p. 91 Miami Herald/MCT/Landov; p. 93 Lilly Echeverria/Miami Herald/MCT via Getty Images; pp. 98, 101, 102 © Bettmann/CORBIS; p. 105 Jorge Castellanos/Orinoquiaphoto; p. 108 EUGENE GARCIA/AFP/Getty Images; p. 114 AP Photo/Kyodo News; p. 117 JUNG YEON-JE/AFP/Getty Images; p. 125 Bride Lane Library/Popperfoto/Getty Images.

Contents

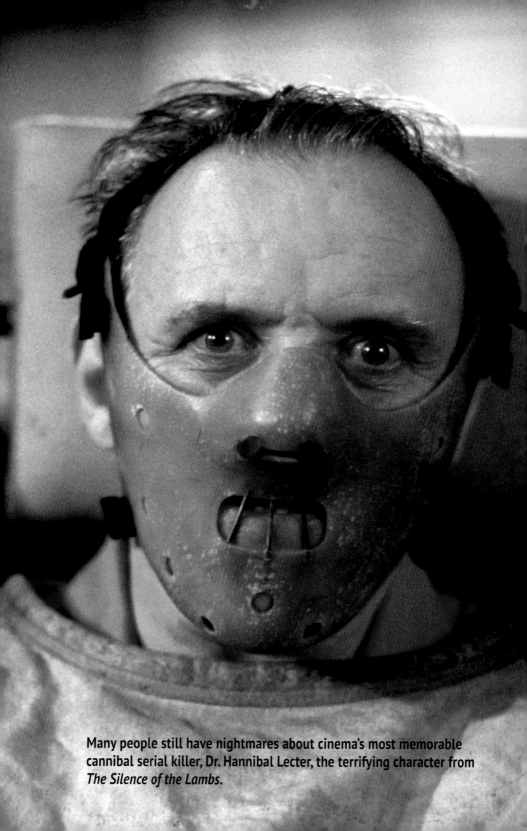

Many people still have nightmares about cinema's most memorable cannibal serial killer, Dr. Hannibal Lecter, the terrifying character from *The Silence of the Lambs*.

INTRODUCTION

"I could eat you up" – people usually think nothing of using that phrase, seeing it just as a expression of appreciation, a colorful way to say that you think a person is cute or nice. Doting grandmothers and adoring lovers most likely have no intention to follow through on what is, if taken literally, a rather horrible proposition: eating another human being. Yet there are people who have done what most would consider unthinkable. Cannibalism is one of the last remaining taboos.

As gruesome as the subject matter is, because of this eerie fascination it has carved out a place in entertainment: It is no longer the domain of horror movie afficionados either, as the infamous Dr. Lecter, Hannibal the Cannibal, has made the jump from novel to silver screen to small screen, and zombies are craving for human flesh across all media from movies to video and board games.

But it is not only the fictional man-eaters that garner a lot of attention. Among the real-life killers that win notoriety for their violent acts, those who cannibalized their victims—or at least are believed to have done so—are probably the ones that are most prominent in the minds of the wider populace. Cannibal serial killers like Fritz Haarmann, Andrei Chikatilo, Ed Gein, or Jeffrey Dahmer are household names in the respective areas of the world where they committed their crimes.

When such a series of murders is unveiled the level of interest is high, the media coverage usually extensive, and sometimes the killers are commemorated in jokes, nursery rhymes, and songs. For example, a song popular in Germany in the 1920s got new lyrics dealing with the murders committed by Haarmann that translated to: "Wait, wait just a little while/then Haarmann will come for you too /With his small cleaver/he will turn you into mincemeat." Another example is a version of "A Visit from St. Nicholas" starring Ed Gein rather than Santa Claus. This dark rendition began, "'Twas the night before Christmas, and all through the shed/All the creatures were stirring, even old Ed/The bodies were hung from the rafters above/While Eddie was searching for another new love."

This kind of humor seems callous, but making light of the horror is a way to deal with fear. And clever songs and rhymes ensure that the memory of these horrors live on, just like the evocative nicknames journalists are eager to come up with for the killers. They are called ghoul, or vampire, or werewolf, but they are far more real than those mythological beasts. Far more frightening, they are human, which prompts the questions that lie at the heart of the fascination with cannibal serial killers: Why do they do it? What can bring a person to commit such heinous crimes?

Chapter 1

A HISTORY OF CANNIBALISM

The word "cannibal" comes from the Spanish language and is said to have originated with Christopher Columbus. When he reached the New World in 1492, Columbus was told by the indigenous people he encountered, the Arawak or Taíno, that their neighbors were man-eaters. These people were called Caribs, and the word "cannibal" derives from their name.[1]

While the name might have been new, the concept of cannibalism, of course, was not. Prior to the popularization of the new term, the practice had been referred to as "anthropophagia" (in Latin; "anthropophagy" in English), derived from the Greek "anthropos": human being, and "phagein": to eat, and a person practicing anthropophagy was called an anthropophagus or, anglicized, an anthropophagite. That is quite a mouthful, and it is no wonder that the new term became more widespread, although the older nomenclature is still used occasionally.

Merriam-Webster's Dictionary defines a cannibal as "one that eats the flesh of its own kind,"[2] that is a human eating human flesh, or an animal eating another animal of the same species. This definition might be a bit too narrow since the consumption of the ashes of a person who was cremated can be seen as an act of cannibalism as well. It is not easy to find a dividing line, though, as calling the consumption of anything that comes from a human body cannibalism would be too broad a definition. Most would probably not consider biting (and swallowing) one's nails to be cannibalistic. Nor is a baby who drinks from his mother's milk commonly thought of as a cannibal, although this way of sucking nourishment from another human being has been likened to vampirism. The drinking of blood is usually seen as a different phenomenon than cannibalism, although they sometimes go hand in hand, and examples of vampirism are included in this book.

A Dog-Eat-Dog World: Cannibalism Among Animals

While eating the flesh of another human being is one of the last remaining taboos in our society, it would be false to call cannibalism unnatural, because it can be observed in nature. From bacteria to higher animals, cannibalism is a widespread phenomenon. It can be differentiated between passive cannibalism, the eating of carrion from the same species, also called necrophagy (from the Greek "nekrós," dead, and "phagein," to eat), which for example can be found in hyenas, and active cannibalism, which involves killing the other animal first. When there is no other food available, animals resort to killing and eating others of their own kind as a strategy for survival. They will feed on their own young who would not be

8

Cannibalism is a regular part of the animal kingdom. Some animals eat the flesh of their friends and relatives when there is no other food source available. Others do it to help out their young.

able to survive anyway if the parents starved, thus ensuring that the older animals can procreate again once the time of scarcity is over.

It is not always hunger that leads animals to commit acts of cannibalism, though. Male lions sometimes kill and eat the offspring of other males to increase the chances of survival and procreation of their own young. Animals in zoos have been observed committing cannibalism, especially mothers eating their young, which is blamed on the stress of captivity. The same is true for pigs and poultry, which are kept in high density in factory farming. But chimpanzees in the wild have also been observed occasionally killing and eating one of their own kind although there were other sources of food available. So far no explanation of this behavior has been found. And some animal species, mainly spiders and insects, exhibit sexual cannibalism, in which the female devours the male after or even while in the process of mating to get specific nutrients that help in the development of their offspring.[3]

Beset by Hunger

Just like there are several different situations in which cannibalism can arise in the animal kingdom, there exist a number of conceivable motives for humans to consume others of their kind. The first that comes to mind is hunger.

There are documented cases of cannibalism committed out of hunger, where people had to resort to eating their companions to ensure their own survival. One famous example is that of Uruguayan Air Force Flight 571, which crashed in the Andes in 1972. The plane had been chartered by the Christian Brothers, a catholic rugby team, and was on its way to bring the team and its supporters to a match in Chile. Eight days after the crash the survivors heard on the radio that the search had been called off because they were thought to be dead. Eight of the twenty-five people who had survived the crash were killed by an avalanche two weeks later. Since there was no rescue coming, they sent out expeditions to find help. It took more than two months before the survivors were finally rescued, which they survived in the harsh conditions high up in the mountains by feeding on those who perished in the disaster after their limited supplies ran out.

Another well-known example is the Donner party, a group of pioneers who got snowed in on their way to California in the Sierra Nevada Mountains in the winter of 1846 to 1847 and survived by eating the dead, although there are some doubts that all who were

When a plane carrying a Uruguayan rugby team crashed in the Andes Mountains in 1972, the survivors turned to cannibalism when their supplies were depleted.

eaten died of natural causes. There are comparable instances of cannibalism throughout history, whether it came after a shipwreck or in a particularly dire situation in war, for example, the Battle of Stalingrad that raged from August 1942 to February 1943, in which first the city and the defending Russians were cut off from supplies, before the attacking German forces were surrounded, leading to occurrences of cannibalism on both sides.

What all of these cases have in common is that they happened in desperate situations as a last resort where cannibalism was the only way for people to survive, and it is not disputed that this has happened occasionally. What is debatable, though, is the existence of a different form of culinary cannibalism that is not forced by hopeless circumstances, but rather a decision to fall back on human flesh for nourishment although there are other sources of food available. Many people who hear the word "cannibal" probably have a picture in their head of primitive tribesmen in a dark jungle on a remote island in a far-off corner of the world hunting other humans, sometimes referred to as "long pig" to dehumanize them, to eat, or of unfortunate missionaries sitting in the oversized cooking pots of the savages they wanted to convert.

These mental pictures have a basis in fiction rather than fact; they are fueled by adventure stories like Robinson Crusoe, and these motifs have become so widespread that many will accept them as the truth, although some anthropologists are now convinced that this form of cannibalism never existed. In the nineteenth century researchers were eager to interpret findings of human remains from prehistoric times that were missing body parts or where the bones were broken as a sign that cannibalism had taken place, often not considering that the remains might have been damaged long after death, and that their placement and preparation could be the consequence of specific funerary rites rather than anthropophagy. Anthropologists at the time tended to compare the way of life of indigenous, "primitive" peoples with that of prehistoric humans, and since they were convinced that the latter were cannibals, so it was assumed the former were as well.[4]

A Worldview of Cannibalism

It is likely that these expectations to encounter cannibalism have their roots in a prejudice that existed for millennia. Since ancient

Treacherous conditions befell the Donner party on their way to
California. Stuck in the Sierra Nevada Mountains with limited
resources, they ate the flesh of their dead to survive.

times cannibalism was seen as a dividing line between civilization and barbarism.

The Greek historian Herodotus (c. 484 BCE to c. 425 BCE) is often called "pater historiae" ("father of history") because he scrutinized his material and named his sources, setting an important example for the historians that came after him. In his only surviving work, *The Histories*, Herodotus recounts the history of the known world from roughly the year 700 BCE to 479 BCE, which includes descriptions of various peoples, and it is noticeable that these get more outlandish the further they lived from his native Greece. According to Herodotus, the Scythians living north of the Black Sea drank the blood of the enemies they killed in battle, and their heads were kept as trophies. The Massagetae living on the steppes of Central Asia allegedly offered their old as a sacrifice before cooking and eating their remains. They shared this practice of ritual cannibalism with the Issedones.

The Padaei of India were said to sacrifice and eat their ill as well as the few who reached old age, and the Androphagi (from "androi," men, and "phagein," to eat) living north of the Scythians Herodotus considered, much as the name suggests, the most savage as they had no laws and were cannibals. The standard of civilization drops the further Herodotus's description goes from his center of the world: The outskirts are populated by monsters like headless men in Northern Africa and the one-eyed Arimaspi somewhere north of the Issedones.

While Herodotus himself expressed some doubts about the accuracy of these reports—and it is understandable that the quality of his sources decreased with the increase in distance to the peoples being described—many took them at face value. Other authors added to the descriptions of the odd human-like creatures living at the edge of the world and their strange customs, and their existence was widely accepted as fact as evidenced by medieval maps like the Hereford Mappa Mundi, an illustration of the world 52 inches (132 centimeters) in diameter dating from the late thirteenth century, that record the location of various monstrous races.[5]

When European explorers started to travel around the world, they took their preconceived notions with them, and it is more than likely that their observation of customs foreign to them were colored by their expectations of what they would find. It is noteworthy, though, that some of the people they encountered held similar notions about the visitors coming from faraway lands. Portuguese traders coming to China were suspected of abducting and eating children.[6] Scottish explorer David Livingstone who traveled through Africa in the middle of the nineteenth century remarked: "Most writers believe the blacks to be savages; nearly all blacks believe the whites to be cannibals. The nursery hobgoblin of the one is black, of the other white."[7] The one thing all humans seem to have in common is the fear of what we do not know, which leads to those outside of one's own culture being viewed with mistrust. And it is not necessary to travel far for that; minorities often came under suspicion of cannibalism as part of unholy rituals.

The accusation of cannibalism, unfounded as it may be, is a powerful and frequently used weapon to degrade groups of people, making them out to be despicable barbarians rather than civilized human beings deserving to be treated as equals. Perhaps European explorers found cannibals everywhere not only because they expected them to be there, but also because it was convenient for

Stories of white missionaries being captured and cannibalized
while attempting to "civilize" certain cultures, as in this depiction of
Franciscans being dismembered and devoured by Caribbean Indians,
horrified many who believed they were providing a noble service.

them as an excuse, allowing them to see and treat the people they denounced as man-eating savages and inferiors.

Motives for Cannibalism

It is possible that explorers confused the dried limbs of monkeys with those of humans, or that they simply misunderstood statements from the people they encountered.[8] In some cases, what seemed like cannibalistic rituals were purely symbolic, which might have been unclear to people not familiar with the customs. Communication cannot have been easy without a common language, leaving lots of room for interpretation, which was influenced by preconceived notions about cannibalism.

Although cannibalism likely was never as widespread as some accounts from the early modern period make it out to be, the opposing view held by some anthropologists that anthropophagy never existed apart from occasional cases of survival cannibalism is probably overstated as well, as there are indications that it was practiced in some cultures. It is important to consider the reasons cannibalism is practiced, though. Hunger as a motive is generally believed to be a myth aside from rare cases of extreme necessity, but there are other motivations.

When looking at cannibalism as a cultural practice, there is a distinction between exocannibalism and endocannibalism, depending on who gets eaten. Endocannibalism is a form of cannibalism in which a person from the same community is consumed, while exocannibalism is the practice of eating a person who does not belong to the same community.

The choice of who gets eaten reflects the motive for cannibalism. Endocannibalism is usually thought of as a ritualistic practice linked

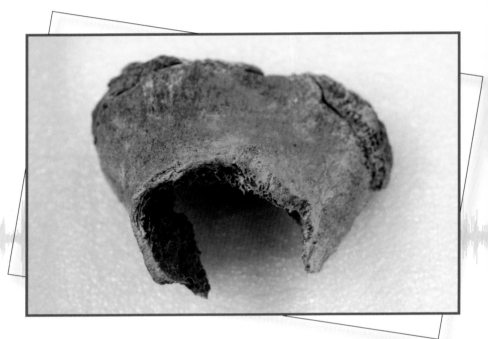

Forensic evidence from skull and bone fragments found at the site of the Jamestown colony suggest that starving colonists resorted to cannibalism during an especially brutal winter. Experts believe that after one teenage girl's death, colonists consumed her flesh and organs.

to funerary customs. Consuming the flesh of the deceased allows the bereaved to keep a part of the lost loved one and helps them grieve. Exocannibalism on the other hand is practiced as a way to celebrate the victory over an enemy, possibly in the hope of gaining part of their strength or some other positive characteristic. It can also be understood as an insult (not least because what has been eaten will inevitably be excreted).

A third form of cannibalism, in which a person eats a part of their own body, is called autocannibalism or self-cannibalism. To a small degree this happens naturally as dead cells from the mouth region are consumed unwittingly and unavoidably. Eating a larger part of one's own body is usually a symptom of a mental disorder, or a form of torture when a person is forced to consume part of themselves against their will. One form of autocannibalism that seems to have gained some popularity in recent years in the United States is placentophagy, eating the afterbirth following childbirth. Many mammals do this, even herbivores, because of the nutritional value, which is not a concern for most people in the Western world, but some believe in the health benefits of eating the placenta, and the organ has been used for a long time in traditional Chinese medicine as well as by other peoples around the world.

Medicinal cannibalism has existed all throughout history. In ancient Rome, the blood of Gladiators was believed to be a cure for epilepsy, and even in the nineteenth century people still tried to obtain the blood of executed prisoners, fresh from the decapitated body, to heal the falling sickness.[9] In the sixteenth and seventeenth centuries, corpse medicine was booming in Europe, where powdered Egyptian mummies and other human remains were added to elixirs and human fat was used as a salve, while at the same time Native Americans and other "primitive" peoples were condemned for cannibalism.[10]

Of course these cures emerged from homeopathic ideas and did not have a scientific basis, so the distinction between medicinal and magical cannibalism is largely arbitrary, as both forms of anthropophagy aim to produce an effect without regard to natural causality. Witches were believed to use human blood and body parts in their concoctions to practice their evil magic, and the connection between witches and cannibalism is seen in fairy tales like that of

Cannibal Serial Killers

While historians can't agree on how common cannibalism was in many cultures around the world, it is believed that eating the flesh of conquered enemies was practiced as a ritualistic ceremony. In this 1781 engraving, Maipure Indians grill the legs of a dead enemy.

Hansel and Gretel, who have to escape from a witch planning to eat them. The belief in other supernatural creatures like vampires and werewolves may in part have been inspired by actual cases of people drinking the blood and eating the flesh of others, as the pathological cannibalism and vampirism seen in some serial killers is not a modern phenomenon. Such occurrences have been recorded for centuries, but it is a relatively recent idea to give serious thought on what might drive a person to such extremes.

Chapter 2

SERIAL MURDER AND CANNIBALISM

There have been numerous definitions of serial murder put forward over the last few decades to distinguish it from other types of murderous crime. While the specifics differ, there are some similarities in these attempts to succinctly describe this phenomenon.

Murder is defined as the unlawful killing of another human being, excluding for example killing in self-defense, which is classified as lawful. Obviously, there has to be more than one murder for it to be considered serial murder. These multiple murders have to be committed by the same person or group of people to have a combining factor (although it is relatively rare that a series of murders is committed by more than one person). There are, however, forms of multiple murder committed by the same offender(s) that are not considered to be serial killings. A double or triple homicide that occurs at a single location within a short period of time does not

The Types and Behaviors of Serial Killers

	Organized	Disorganized
IQ	105–120 (falls within normal range)	80–95 (below average)
Social skills	Normal	Poor
Childhood	Grew up with a stable father or father figure; may have encountered physical abuse	Grew up with an abusive father or no father present; may have encountered emotional abuse
Proximity of murders to home	Moves around a lot to flee murder scenes	Commits murders around home
Living situation	Married, lives with partner, or dates	Lives alone, doesn't date
Education	Possibly attended college	Dropped out of high school
Time of activity	Daytime	Nighttime
Method of ensnaring victims	Seduction	Attack
Interaction with victims	Converses with victims	Does not consider victims to be people
Method of disposal	May dismember body after killing; disposes of remains	Leaves body behind after killing; usually does not dismember
State of crime scene	Controlled; little physical evidence left behind	Chaotic; leaves physical evidence behind
Reason for returning to scene of crime	To see the police working; interest in police work	To relive the murder

Source: O'Connor, Tom. "Serial Killer Typology."
http://www.ravenndragon.net/montgomery/csi/oconnortypology1.pdf

fall in the category of serial murder, and neither do mass murders, in which four or more people are killed during an event. Similarly, spree killings in which the offender kills more than one person in a period of time that can span several days but without remaining in the same location are not considered serial murder either.

The element of time separates serial murder from these other forms of multiple murders. For it to be considered serial murder, the murders have to occur in separate events, which can but don't have to happen in the same location. Some time has to pass between these events, though, which is sometimes referred to as a cooling-off period.

The definition put forward by the Federal Bureau of Investigation (FBI) describes serial murder as the "unlawful killing of two or more victims by the same offender(s), in separate events."[1] This definition is deliberately kept simple by not going into the possible motivations for serial murder, which complicate things considerably and have to be looked at separately.

Myths About Serial Killers

According to the FBI, there are several myths and misconceptions in regard to serial killers. For most people, serial murder is a topic they encounter solely in novels and movies, and one has to keep in mind that those are produced for entertainment purposes and are therefore more concerned with telling a compelling story rather than being accurate in portraying how serial murder actually happens. Hence, it is necessary to question any preconceived notions one might have in regard to serial murder to be able to look at real cases objectively.

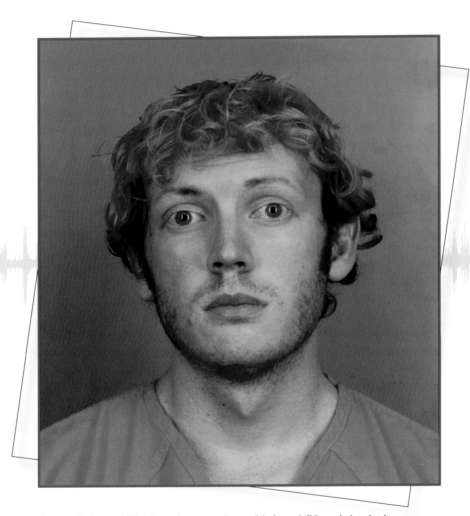

James Holmes killed twelve people and injured fifty-eight during a shooting spree at a Colorado movie theater in 2012. Holmes is considered a mass murderer, not a serial killer.

But it is not only the influence of the media that can leave its mark; investigators can be influenced by their experience with previous cases, which might stand in the way of an unbiased treatment of future cases. Human beings are complicated beasts, their histories and motivations can differ wildly, which is why it is important to not rely too much on stringent classifications, although they can be helpful, and see every case as unique to keep an open mind.[2]

One common myth is that serial killers are "reclusive, social misfits who live alone."[3] Looking at the cases presented in this book, there are some who fit the description, for example, Karl Denke or Ed Gein, but there are also others who led a (relatively) normal family life like Peter Kürten or Andrei Chikatilo, whose crimes, when finally uncovered, came as a shock even to their wives.

The second myth listed by the FBI, that serial killers are all white males, is influenced by a US-centric view. Not all serial murders in the United States are committed by whites, and there are serial murders in countries where the population is not predominantly white. The next chapter will look at cases from all over the world, including cannibalistic killings committed by natives of Venezuela, Japan, and South Korea. It is equally untrue that only men become serial killers, although the number of women is much smaller. The estimates differ regarding how many serial killers are women, ranging from 5–8 to 10–15 percent.[4]

The misconception that there are no female serial killers was probably influenced by the low percentage, as well as the fact that for a long time men considered the "gentler sex" incapable of such crimes. Additionally, women tend to kill in ways that attract less attention as they usually do not rely on physical violence, poison being the weapon of choice for a majority of female serial killers.[5] Yet there are a few rare cases of female cannibal killers, a crime that could not be more physical.

The commonly held belief that all serial killers travel to commit their crimes in a greater geographical area is contradicted as well by the examples in this book. Most murdered close to home, and those who operated in a greater area traveled for reasons other than finding victims, for example, the requirements of their job, and the killing merely coincided with their traveling.

Anyone who thinks women can't be serial killers has never heard of Aileen Wuornos, who killed seven men in the span of a year.

Contrary to the widely held notion that serial killers cannot stop killing once they have started and that their crimes will only stop when they are caught, there are some who take breaks between their murders that are years long, and sometimes they even stop altogether, either because their circumstances prevent them from killing or they find activities that work as a substitute.[6]

Not all serial killers are insane. "As a group, serial killers suffer from a variety of personality disorders, including psychopathy, anti-social personality, and others. Most, however, are not adjudicated as insane under the law."[7] Many of the murderers presented in the next chapter showed signs of mental health problems before they started killing, yet in several cases they were found to be not insane by the court, meaning that they were considered to be in control of their actions and aware of the consequences of their doing, despite any personality disorders.

Serial killers are not all evil geniuses, either, which seems to be a particularly popular archetype in fiction. A good example is the most famous fictional cannibal serial killer, Dr. Hannibal Lecter, whose superior intellect makes him a formidable foe for law enforcement. There is no information available regarding the intelligence quotient (IQ) of all the real killers presented in the next chapter, but three of them, Fritz Haarmann, Joachim Kroll, and Ottis Toole, were found to be of well-below-average intelligence. Edmund Kemper on the other hand nearly reached genius level in an IQ test, but still his crimes were not akin to the Machiavellian schemes authors construct for their brilliant villains to enthrall readers and moviegoers.

It is a myth that serial killers want to get caught, although the behavior of some seems to suggest it. According to the FBI, serial

Unlike "Hannibal the Cannibal," most serial killers do not have unusually high IQs.

killers can become overconfident when they have been able to operate without being caught for some time, which leads them to not being as careful when committing their crimes and to taking chances: "It is not that serial killers want to get caught; they feel that they can't get caught."[8] That does not only apply to the acts of murder, but also to the killers' behavior afterwards, as some apparently have the urge to glory in their deeds after the fact. Edmund Kemper hung around cop bars and discussed the murders he had committed with the unsuspecting officers, Peter Kürten frequently returned to the scenes of his crimes, Albert Fish and Tsutomu Miyazaki sent letters to the families of their victims, risks that could have led (and, in the case of Fish, did lead) to their arrest.

Finally, it is a myth that sex is the only motivation for serial killers. What other motivations can drive people to kill will be looked at in greater detail below.

What Makes a Killer?

Many people can imagine a situation in which they would act violently, and maybe find themselves thinking at some point in their life "I could kill him/her." But they never act on the impulse, treating it as a thought born out of anger or frustration that might even scare them since they did not consider themselves capable of such a thing. How is it that some people do act upon the impulse to kill, and do so repeatedly?

A genetic predisposition has been considered as the reason, but so far no gene has been identified as being responsible for criminal behavior. Other potential physiological causes have been looked at as well, and it seems common that serial killers suffered head trauma while growing up. Many suffer from some form of epilepsy, and it is speculated that a malfunction of the hypothalamus is to blame. There is no reliable evidence for this, though, and a lot more serial killers would have to be examined to see if any part of their brains can be isolated as the responsible factor for their acts.[9] Early attempts to find any abnormity of the brain of a serial killer as in the case of Fritz Haarmann after his execution in 1925 did not yield any result, but of course science has advanced greatly since then, and future research might be able to identify physiological factors that are still unknown.

What drives serial killers to act is a subject still under debate. Scientists have studied the brains of serial killers, including these sections from John Wayne Gacy's brain, in an attempt to find common traits.

While a physiological trait characteristic of serial killers, if one were discovered, would likely be easy to test for, psychological factors are more complicated. The number of influences on the development of a person is countless, and it is not clear what causes antisocial and violent behavior. Many serial killers suffered neglect and abuse in their childhood, but not all did. And of course not every neglected or abused child grows up to be a serial killer. Hence, it is believed that it is not a single factor, but rather a rare combination of factors, which leads to the development of a serial killer.

A certain biological predisposition in conjunction with social and environmental influences at a critical time in a person's development can lead to that person becoming a serial killer. And while it is an uncomfortable truth that it is impossible to identify all of the factors leading to that result and therefore we do not know how to prevent it from happening, it is important to remember that the "most significant factor is the serial killer's personal decision in choosing to pursue their crimes."[10] No one is doomed by their genetic material or their upbringing to end up as a serial killer, and no killer is excused for their crimes because of these factors.

Classification of Serial Killers

The causes that lead to the development of a serial killer may be impossible to identify, but the specific motivations of serial killers are not.

What drives a person to murder another human being? Anger, greed, jealousy, revenge, the desire to keep something secret ... there are many possible motives. Usually the reason becomes apparent when looking at the connection between murderer and

One common experience in most serial killers is the presence or threat of abuse in the home during childhood. It is important to remember, however, that all children who suffer or witness abuse do not grow up

victim. In many cases, murderer and victim know each other, and the motive arises out of their personal relationship.

In that respect, most serial killers differ from other murderers as usually offender and victim do not know each other before the murder, and the murderer's motivation is not influenced by any personal connection with the victim. This lack of a link between murderer and victim makes the killer difficult to catch.

A commonly used tool for the categorization of serial killers based on their motivation is the Holmes typology. First put forward by Ronald M. Holmes and James E. De Burger in 1988 and later refined by Holmes and his son, Stephen T. Holmes, this typology is based on interviews given by serial killers about the reasons why they kill. Resting on that material, serial murderers are divided into four different categories: Visionary, Mission, Hedonistic, and Power/Control.

Visionary killers are influenced by visions or voices they hear, which urge them to kill. These killers are psychotic, suffering from a loss of their sense of reality.

Killers in the second category believe they are on a mission to eliminate a defined group of victims, to rid the world of certain people the killer considers to be undesirable.

Hedonistic serial killers do it because they enjoy killing or because of some other gain. Killers in this category derive pleasure from having power over a person to the point where they decide whether the victim lives or dies.[11]

Hedonistic killers are further divided into three subcategories: comfort (or profit) killers, thrill killers, and lust killers.

Comfort killers are after material gain, and this category includes female serial killers, colloquially called black widows, who

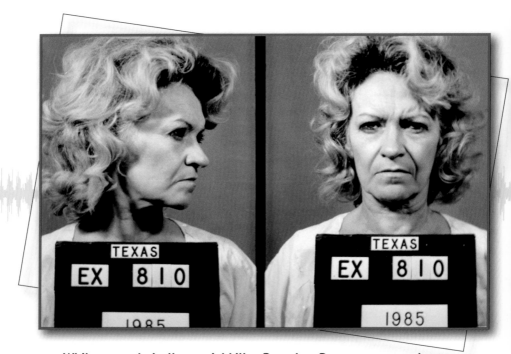

While not technically a serial killer, Betty Lou Beets came very close. Known as a "black widow," Beets attempted to murder her second and third husbands, and she succeeded with her fourth and fifth husbands.

kill their partners or family members for an inheritance or to claim life insurance benefits. The male equivalent to the black widow killer is the bluebeard killer, named after a French folktale about a nobleman who murdered his wives. Hitmen who kill for profit fall into this category as well.

Thrill killers murder for the rush they get from committing the crime, but also from the chase, and they will often send messages to the investigators, taunting them or boasting about their deeds.

Lust killers are probably the largest group among serial killers, as shown by the fact that the FBI deems it necessary to make clear that it is a myth that serial killers are only motivated by sex. Many are, however, and the sexual acts committed by the offenders are not necessarily restricted to conventional sexual practices but can also include what is known as paraphilias (unusual sexual interests), which include cannibalism and vampirism.

As a consequence, it is to be suspected that most cannibal serial killers fall into the category of lust killers.

Chapter 3

EXAMPLES OF CANNIBAL SERIAL KILLERS

"I send you half the Kidne I took from one women prasarved it for you tother piece I fried and ate it was very nise [...]."[1] This is part of a letter known after its stated place of dispatch as "From Hell," which is attributed to Jack the Ripper, the unidentified serial killer who murdered and mutilated at least five prostitutes in London's East End in 1888. The letter arrived with part of a kidney, which was identified as human, but it is unclear if it was taken from one of the murder victims or if it was a hoax like hundreds of letters sent to law enforcement and newspapers at the time.

Jack the Ripper was not the first serial killer, but he was the first whose deeds created a media frenzy, which is why the case is so widely known and people are still trying to solve the mysteries surrounding the murders and identify the culprit. Whether Jack cannibalized his victims or not, because of the "From Hell" letter, cannibalism was connected to serial murder from the time it was perceived by a wider public, and the cases of serial killers who consume parts of their victims still seem to attract the most attention.

Erzsébet Báthory
aka "The Bloody Countess"

Born: **August 7, 1560**
Profession: **Noblewoman**
Motive: **Sadism**
Arrested: **December 29, 1610**
Died: **August 21, 1614**

Countess Erzsébet (anglicized: Elizabeth) Báthory has the dubious honor of being recognized by the *Guinness Book of World Records* as the murderess who claimed the most victims. She is supposed to have killed 650 girls and young women.

Elizabeth was born on August 7, 1560 to one of the wealthiest and most powerful noble families of Hungary. Her parents came from different branches of the same family, a political move to bring together opposing factions of the noble house of Báthory. Marriages of this kind were a way to keep the family fortune intact, but they may also have had negative effects. Several of her relatives were said to be degenerates, and Elizabeth supposedly suffered from epilepsy, possibly a result of this practice of inbreeding among noble families. Little is known about Elizabeth's childhood except that she was educated well, as she was able to read and write in four languages. There are stories claiming that she witnessed brutal torture while she was still very young, which would not be unusual for a child from

Elizabeth Báthory tortured and killed hundreds of girls.

a noble family at the time. She was engaged to Frenec Nádasdy, who was four years older than she, at age eleven and married to him in 1575. In the war against the Turks, Nádasdy made a name for himself. He was called the Black Knight, and he earned a reputation of cruelty. He is supposed to have taught his wife some torturing techniques.

While her husband was away at war, Elizabeth stayed at home to manage the family estate and to look after her five children, only three of whom lived into adulthood. After her husband's death she was determined not to be exploited like many widows were, but to rule with the same strength as would be expected from a man. Allegedly she had a distinct masculine side since her youth, enjoying typically male activities like hunting, and preferring male clothing, but it is unknown how much of this falls into the realm of legend.

The same is true about the abuse and the murders that allegedly started after her husband's death, as there were no reports of any crimes before the investigation began in 1610. Elizabeth Báthory was accused of luring peasant girls into her castle, who she whipped or beat with sticks and tortured with needles and hot metal objects. Purportedly she liked biting the girls and tearing the flesh from their bones, experiencing ectasy by the sight of blood. The bodies were left to rot under beds in the castle or thrown into the fields outside. The act she is most (in)famous for, bathing in the blood of virgins to achieve eternal life and beauty, is demonstrably a later invention, though.

The authorities only stepped in after the Bloody Countess started to claim girls from noble families as her victims as well. She was arrested shortly before the turn of the year 1610, and in January

1611 Elizabeth was sentenced to imprisonment. While her servants, who had confessed of the crimes, were burned alive as her accomplices, Elizabeth was confined to her bedchamber; the windows of which were walled up. She died there in 1614.[2]

In the story of the Bloody Countess it is difficult to tell fact from fiction: Many legends and folktakes grew around her, to which novels and movies are added even to this day. Historian Tony Thorne came to the conclusion that the charges against Elizabeth Báthory were likely made up by people who were after her lands and money, although he admits that it is impossible to say for certain whether she committed these horrendous crimes or not.[3]

Danger signs

Unknown

Pattern of crime

Abducting and torturing girls

Number of victims

Approximately 650

Karl Denke

Born: **February 11, 1860**
Profession: **None**
Motive: **Unknown**
Arrested: **December 21, 1924**
Died: **December 22, 1924 (suicide)**

On December 21, 1924 a beggar came to the door of Karl Denke in Münsterberg, Silesia (part of Germany at the time, today Ziębice, Poland). Denke asked him in, telling him that he could earn a little money by writing down a letter for him. Denke began to dictate, but when the beggar turned away from the sheet of paper to inquire if he had heard correctly, he saw that Denke was about to hit him in the head with a pickax. Instead of having his skull caved in, he only took a glancing blow to the temple, and he was able to flee. His cries alerted the neighbors, but reporting the attack to the police resulted in the victim being placed under arrest for begging.

Denke was brought in for questioning later that day, and after contradicting himself he was put in a cell as well, where he strangulated himself with a handkerchief during the night. The reason for the suicide of the seemingly peaceful if odd and tight-lipped man who was referred to as "Papa Denke" and always seemed to have a place

Karl Denke regularly took in vagrants to provide them—and himself—with a meal. Denke wasn't wasteful: whatever parts of the bodies he didn't consume, he used as implements.

to stay and a meal for vagrants became apparent when his apartment was searched. A barrel full of cured meat and other pieces prepared as food were found to be human flesh.

Denke was born on February 11, 1860, in the village of Kunzendorf near Münsterberg to a reasonably well-off farmer. As a boy he was extremely withdrawn, a trait that charactized Denke his whole life, and even refused to speak until he was seven or eight years old. He ran away from home twice, but returned months later without offering an explanation. He seemed emotionless and apathetic; a teacher considered him to be mentally challenged.

In 1880 he moved into the house in Münsterberg where he later committed his crimes. Denke kept a record of his murders, which was found in a book under his bed. From 1903 on he had documented thirty murders, noting the date as well as the name, birthday, and hometown of the victims. Additionally, he kept a tally of the slaughter weight of the people he killed. His victims included men and women, ranging from sixteen to seventy-six years of age, but the majority were men above age forty.

Denke not only cooked and ate his victims, he also turned their remains into objects of daily use. He had made suspenders, shoelaces, and straps from human skin; the latter he used when weaving baskets that he sold. The bones and teeth of the murder victims he collected in a shed a few steps away from his house, cleaned and sorted neatly.

Afterwards it came out that his neighbors had occasionally heard butchering noises from his apartment and noticed a rotting smell, and they had seen Denke dispose of buckets of blood or go into the woods with a handbarrow loaded with sacks, but they did not think anything of it. Denke professed that he was slaughtering

Inside Denke's apartment and nearby shed, investigators discovered cooking pots and jars, as well as some bones and other remains from his victims. These findings were chillingly neat and tidy.

rabbits and dogs to get some meat, which was hard to come by at the time, and a few people came forward to report that they had bought meat from him, although it is doubtful that it came from goats like he claimed. It had also been observed that men fled from Denke's apartment on at least two occasions, but they did not go to the police. Denke was careful to choose victims that came from out of town and would not be missed immediately, and the police probably would not have given much credit to vagrants and beggars.

The fact that Denke used skin from the breast including the nipples and from the pubic area to make and repair his suspenders seems to point to a sexual motive for his crimes, but by killing himself he denied investigators an explanation of what drove him to murder and eat his victims.[4]

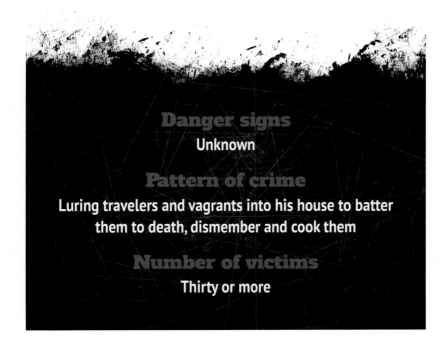

Danger signs

Unknown

Pattern of crime

Luring travelers and vagrants into his house to batter them to death, dismember and cook them

Number of victims

Thirty or more

Enriqueta Martí
aka "The Vampire of Barcelona"

Born: **1868**

Profession: **Brothelkeeper and quack doctor**

Motive: **Greed**

Arrested: **February 27, 1912**

Died: **May 12, 1913**

Children had been disappearing in Barcelona, Spain, for years. In February 1912, a neighbor thought she saw a girl that fit the description of the latest abduction victim, Teresita Guitart Congost, in the apartment of Enriqueta Martí, and on the twenty-seventh of the month the police went to investigate. Found in the apartment were two little girls, the missing Teresita, who had been lured away from her home with the promise of candy, and Angelita, whose statements told of graver crimes their captor had committed.

The girls said that they had discovered a sack containing children's clothing and a knife covered in blood. Angelita stated that she had seen how Martí killed a little boy with a knife on the kitchen table. Police found the sack with bloody clothing, as well as some bones. When searching Enriqueta Martí's other properties, authorities detected more remains of children, including jars that seemingly held the coagulated blood, fat, and powdered bones of her victims.

Enriqueta Martí's murderous ways unraveled when two little girls she was holding captive were able to testify against her. Martí used her murder victims as salves and potions in her work as a witch doctor.

Enriqueta Martí was born in Sant Feliu de Llobregat in 1868, but she moved to nearby Barcelona to work as a maidservant. Later she became a prostitute and brothel keeper, specializing in procuring children for a rich clientele. In 1909, she was arrested for running a brothel catering to pedophiles. She was never tried, though, which led to speculation that she was protected by powerful patrons who had an interest in the case not going to court where their involvement would have been uncovered.

Safe and sound, little Teresita Guitart Congost stands surrounded by the policemen who rescued her.

It is suspected that Martí was active for over ten years, abducting children to prostitute them or to kill them and turn their remains into salves and potions. Allegedly, she was a witch doctor who made quack remedies for tuberculosis and other diseases from the blood and fat of murdered children, which were fetching high prices at a time before the discovery of antibiotics, and some claim that she partook of this gruesome medicine herself. A notebook with recipes for elixirs was found in her apartment, as well as a mysterious pack of cards with ciphers and initials on them, which were believed to point to Martí's clients who were widely speculated about.

Martí attempted suicide by cutting her wrists with a wooden spoon, and measures were taken to prevent her from killing herself. Instead she was lynched by other prisoners, so she never stood trial and the identity of her patrons remained a secret.[5]

Danger signs
Unknown

Pattern of crime
Abducting children to prostitute and/or kill for ingredients used in her quack remedies

Number of victims
Unknown

Albert Fish

"The Boogeyman," "The Brooklyn Vamp
e Werewolf of Wysteria," and "The Gray M

Born: **May 19, 1870**
Profession: **House painter**
Motive: **Sadism**
Arrested: **December, 1930**
Died: **January 16, 1936 (executed)**

n November 1934, an anonymous letter was delivered to the Budd family in New York whose daughter, Grace, had been missing for six years. In this letter Grace's killer described in detail how he had become fascinated by cannibalism and how he had killed and dismembered the twelve-year-old girl to satisfy his urge. The police investigation spurred by the letter led to Albert Fish.

Fish was not unfamiliar to the missing girl's family. He had called upon the Budds on June 3, 1928, claiming to be interested in hiring their son Edward on his farm for the summer. (Edward had posted a newspaper ad seeking such work.) The Budds invited Fish to dinner and then allowed him to take Grace with him, as he said he would take her to a children's birthday party at his sister's house. Instead he took Grace to a deserted cottage in Westchester, where he strangled her and hacked her body apart. He took some of her flesh to his home

Albert Fish lured Grace Budd from her parents' home, murdered her, and feasted on her remains. The demented sadist then taunted the little girl's frantic parents.

Hamilton Fish, who later adopted the name Albert, was born in 1870 in Washington, D.C. His father died when he was only five years old, which led to his mother putting him in an orphanage so she could find work. There Fish and the other children were subjected to physical abuse. Fish later said that he enjoyed getting beaten and seeing the other children get spanked, although this exposure to violence seems to have had a noticeably negative effect that continued even after his mother removed him from the orphanage in 1880. Fish started to stammer, and he had a bed-wetting problem until he was eleven years old.

Fish moved to New York, where he worked as a painter, and he got married in 1898 and had six children, whom he raised alone after his wife left him in 1917. His daughter reported at his trial that he read the Bible, went to church, and never raised a hand to his children. But their family life can hardly be considered normal, as he practiced masochistic behavior like self-flagellation and pushing needles into his body, and he asked his children to beat him with a paddle studded with nails. He was obsessed with violence and torture, and he collected any material he could find about cannibalism, especially about the case of Fritz Haarmann.

According to Fish, his fascination with anthropophagy started when an older brother of his told him stories about cannibalism in the Far East. He also liked to write obscene letters to women whose addresses he got from ads they placed in newspapers. For this he was arrested in December 1930, but he was let go after a psychiatric evaluation came to the conclusion that he was disturbed but not a threat, a rather drastic lapse of judgment as it turned out.

After he was arrested in 1934, Fish claimed to have molested children in every state, possibly more than 400. And he was

Investigators searched the property where Fish had taken Budd. There, they found evidence tying Fish to the little girl's abduction and murder, as well as the molestation, torture, and murder of several other children.

suspected to have killed at least fifteen of them after torturing them brutally, although he confessed only to six, including the killing of a four-year-old boy in 1929, who he also cannibalized. He claimed to hear voices that called on him to commit his crimes, and he was convinced that he was doing God's will.

Fish was put on trial for the kidnapping and murder of twelve-year-old Grace Budd in 1928. Psychiatrists declared him to be abnormal but not insane, and a jury found him guilty. He was sentenced to death and electrocuted on January 16, 1936 at Sing Sing.[6]

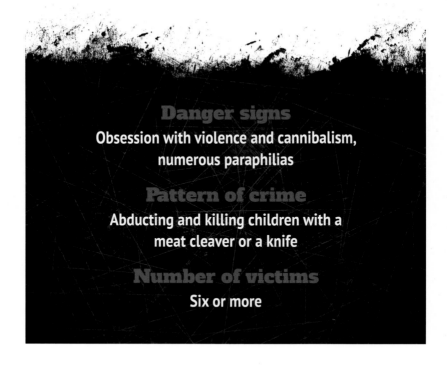

Danger signs

Obsession with violence and cannibalism, numerous paraphilias

Pattern of crime

Abducting and killing children with a meat cleaver or a knife

Number of victims

Six or more

Leonarda Cianciulli
aka "The Soap-Maker of Correggio"

Born: April 14, 1893
Profession: Shopkeeper
Motive: Superstition, greed
Arrested: November 1940
Died: October 15, 1970

Leonarda Cianciulli was born on April 14, 1893 in Montella, a small town east of Napoli, Italy. Her mother let her feel that she was not wanted, and Cianciulli, who suffered from epilepsy, tried to kill herself three times while she was young. In 1914 she married a man her family did not approve of, with whom she moved to Corregio in 1930 after their home had been destroyed by an earthquake.

According to Cianciulli, a fortune-teller told her that all her children would die, and another foretold that there was prison or a mental institution in her future. Cianciulli was pregnant seventeen times, but she miscarried three times, and ten of her children died in infancy. Protecting her surviving children was of capital importance to her, and the superstitious woman started studying magic as a way to do that.

When her eldest son Giuseppe was drafted into the military in 1939, Cianciulli decided that she would sacrifice others to keep him alive. Over the following year, she drugged three older women who

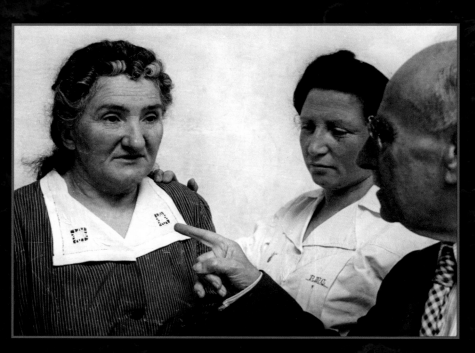

Leonarda Cianciulli used the bodies of her victims to make soaps and pastries. Cianciulli believed her murderous acts were sacrifices that would prevent the deaths of her own children.

had come to her for help, dismembered them with an axe, and used caustic soda to dissolve the remains, which she poured into the septic tank. She collected and dried the blood of her first victim, which she mixed with flour, sugar, chocolate, milk, eggs, and margarine, turning the murdered woman into pastries. These Cianciulli offered to guests, although she and her son ate of them as well. The remains of her third victim she made into soap, earning herself the nickname *la Saponificatrice di Corregio* (the Soap-Maker of Corregio). She gave away the bars of soap to unsuspecting neighbors.

The sister-in-law of Cianciulli's last victim told the police that she had last seen the missing woman going into Cianciulli's house, which led to her arrest in November 1940. Cianciulli was not tried until after World War II. In 1946 she was sentenced to thirty years in prison and three years in a criminal asylum. She died in a mental institution in 1970.[7]

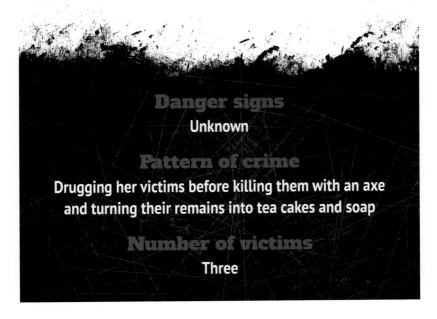

Danger signs

Unknown

Pattern of crime

Drugging her victims before killing them with an axe and turning their remains into tea cakes and soap

Number of victims

Three

Fritz Haarmann
aka *"The Werewolf of Hanover"*

Born: **October 25, 1879**
Profession: **Marketeer**
Motive: **Sadism**
Arrested: **June 22, 1924**
Died: **April 15, 1925 (executed)**

Friedrich Heinrich Karl Haarmann, called Fritz for short, was arrested on June 22, 1924 in his hometown of Hanover, Germany. An underage runaway Haarmann had brought to the police himself told the officers that Haarmann had threatened and abused him, which raised suspicions. In May and June 1924, several human skulls had been found along the banks of the river Leine that flows through the city of Hanover. A thorough search conducted by the police in July turned up so many human remains that there had to have been at least twenty-two victims. Traces of blood were found in Haarmann's apartment, but having no clear evidence the police resorted to unusual methods. Four skulls of young men he was assumed to have killed were put in his cell, burning candles placed behind red paper in their eye sockets. Haunted this way by the souls of the victims, Haarmann confessed.

Haarmann was born on October 25, 1879. He loved his mother dearly but his father, a cantankerous drunkard, he saw as a rival fo

Fritz Haarmann was spooked enough by his own deeds to finally confess. It is believed he sold the flesh of his victims as meat to

the attention of his mother and frequently fought with him. After half a year at officer candidate school in 1895 he was sent home because of a condition referred to as equivalent to epilepsy. In 1896 Haarmann, who had become the victim of sexual abuse at age seven, was sent to an asylum after abusing young boys himself. In 1897 he fled to Switzerland, but returned to Hanover in 1899. The following year he joined the military, but in 1902 he was discharged after he had been diagnosed with a form of mental deficiency. His father tried to have him committed to an insane asylum in 1903, however, an examination ordered by the police came to the conclusion that Haarmann, while of below average intelligence and easily irritable, was not mentally ill. Over the following years he spent a lot of time in jail for theft, fraud, and sex offenses.[8]

In April 1918 he was released after a five-year prison term, and the same year he came under suspicion in the disappearance of a seventeen-year-old. While he was caught with another naked boy, which landed Haarmann in prison once again for nine months, the police did not find anything in Haarmann's apartment relating to the missing person—although the severed head of the boy was hidden behind the stove at the time. Several people voiced their suspicions concerning Haarmann, but to no avail. It is possible that the police were not looking too closely, because Haarmann was working as an informer. In return for his services the police turned a blind eye to Haarmann's petty theft and his activities on the black market, where he earned his livelihood selling used clothes and preserved meat. It is believed that he took both from his victims, and although Haarmann claimed to have disposed of the flesh of his victims in some other way there seems to be no other convincing explanation as to where he might have gotten meat to sell cheaply in the economic hard times after World War I.[9]

Haarmann chose his victims among the boys and young men passing through Hanover in the turmoil after the war, sometimes influenced by his partner, Hans Grans, twenty-two years his younger, who was after the victims' clothes. With the promise of work or at least a meal he lured them into his apartment, demanding sex in return. In ecstasy he choked and bit his victims, tearing out their throats with his teeth and possibly drinking their blood. Then he hacked apart the bodies, stripped the flesh from the bones, and threw them in the river.[10]

The remains of Haarmann's victims were interred together in Stöckener Cemetery. Their names and ages are inscribed on the granite tombstone.

On December 19, 1924, Haarmann was sentenced to death twenty-four times—once for each murder he had been found guilty of. He claimed not to remember the number of his victims, but there were probably more than could be proven. Haarmann was executed by guillotine on April 15, 1925. He was convinced that his crimes would make him so famous that even in a thousand years people would still talk about him. He may have been right about that; due to the media frenzy surrounding the case he is still one of the most widely known serial killers in Germany, and he has been portrayed in numerous books, movies, and even a musical.

Haarmann's head was preserved as an anatomical specimen, which was only cremated in 2014.

Danger signs

History of sexual abuse

Pattern of crime

Biting the throats of his sexual partners

Number of victims

Twenty-four or more

Carl Grossmann

Born: December 13, 1863
Profession: Butcher
Motive: Sadism
Arrested: August 21, 1921
Died: July 4/5, 1922 (suicide)

Carl Friedrich Wilhelm Grossmann was arrested on August 21, 1921 in his apartment in Berlin, after the neighbors had heard screams and called the police. On his bed there was the dead body of a woman, arms tied behind her back, with severe injuries on the face and in the pelvic region. Traces of human blood were found on many of Grossmann's possessions, including several knives and other kitchen utensils, and the ashes in his stove showed that human body parts had been burned in there.

Since 1918 body parts had been found in several bodies of water in Germany's capital. More than twenty women, parts of whose flesh was missing, had been hacked apart and disposed of in this way. Grossmann came under suspicion to be the serial killer the police had been trying to find for some time, and he had even been investigated the year before his arrest when a witness claimed to have recognized him while he was disposing of parts of a dead body, but a search of his apartment did not yield any results at the time.

Carl Grossman murdered twenty or more people, but whether he ate them is debatable. It is believed, however, that he ground some of them into sausage, which he then sold.

When the court proceedings started in July 1922, he was charged with the murder of three women, although estimates of the actual number of his victims are much higher, ranging from twenty to 100 (the high estimate is probably an exaggeration fueled by the press). The extent of his crimes is unclear as Grossmann confessed only to things that could be clearly proven. Therefore, it is equally unknown whether he ate of the flesh of his victims himself but it would not be a surprise in light of his brutal deeds. It is suspected that Grossmann, who for a time operated a stall selling sausage, sold some of the flesh. A witness told the court that Grossmann had offered parts of a dead body to her, which he kept under his bed.

Grossmann was born on December 13, 1863 in Neuruppin, a small town northwest of Berlin, to a poor family. His father, a ragman, was an alcoholic and frequently beat his wife and six children. Grossmann, who was a bad student (although he showed an exceptional memory during the interrogations), left school at age fourteen to work at a cloth mill to help support the family. To get away from his abusive father, Grossmann moved to Berlin when he was sixteen or seventeen, earning money through odd jobs—including working for a butcher, which Grossmann named as his profession during his trial—and petty crime.

He was called upon for military service in 1886 but was discharged the next year because of a sexual offense. Grossmann, who moved to southern Germany after leaving the military, was convicted more than twenty times of various crimes. In 1899 he was sentenced to fifteen years in prison for sexually assaulting a ten-year-old girl and raping a four-year-old so brutally that the girl died shortly after the verdict. After his release he moved back to Berlin where he worked as a peddler.

In the time after World War I there were a lot of poor women looking for a meal and a place to stay, and Grossmann took them in eagerly. During the trial some of those who survived Grossmann's abuse confirmed his extreme sadism, although he claimed to have no such urges. Instead of a sexual motive, he gave outbursts of rage as the reason for his murders, claiming the women had stolen from him or wronged him in some other way. His complete lack of empathy was evident in Grossmann's detailed description of how he dismembered and disposed of the body of one of his victims over the course of several days.

Grossmann eluded the highly probable death penalty by hanging himself in the night from July 4 to July 5, 1922.[11]

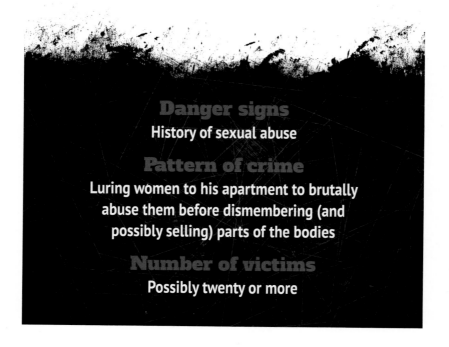

Danger signs

History of sexual abuse

Pattern of crime

Luring women to his apartment to brutally abuse them before dismembering (and possibly selling) parts of the bodies

Number of victims

Possibly twenty or more

Peter Kürten
aka "The Vampire of Düsseldorf"

Born: May 26, 1883
Profession: Unemployed ironfounder
Motive: Sadism
Arrested: May 24, 1930
Died: July 2, 1931 (executed)

Peter Kürten was born on May 26, 1883 in Mülheim near Cologne, Germany. He was one of fourteen children, his father a violent alcoholic who raped his wife in front of the children and was convicted for sexually abusing his thirteen-year-old daughter.

Kürten's sadism became apparent at an early age as he was torturing and killing dogs and farm animals even as a youth, feeling aroused by blood, particularly the sound of blood gushing out of the body he claimed to be able to hear. During his trial he confessed that at the age of nine he had pushed two playmates into a river where they drowned, but the court did not follow up on this. At age sixteen he tried to strangle a girl for the first time.

In 1913 Kürten committed his first verifiable murder, strangling a ten-year-old girl before cutting her throat in the course of a burglary. The crime remained unsolved until Kürten confessed to it seventeen years later.

Peter Kürten, the Vampire of Düsseldorf, murdered at least nine victims. As his nickname suggests, he also drank their blood.

Until 1921 he spent a total of twenty years in prison, for desertion from the military as well as for theft and arson. That year he was released early, because his brother-in-law, a well-off civil servant, had vouched for Kürten, who moved to Altenburg to live with his sister and her family. There he met his future wife, Auguste. She had spent four years in prison herself for manslaughter; in 1911 she had killed her fiancé when he wanted to leave her for another woman after an eight-year engagement. They got married in 1923, but the marriage was strained by Kürten's constant affairs. The couple moved to Düsseldorf in 1925, where Kürten later committed his murders.

Between February 1929 and May 1930 he terrorized the area, strangling his victims, mainly girls and young women, and stabbing them with a pair of scissors or a dagger. Others he attacked with a hammer. Since he usually struck at night and it appeared that he drank some of the blood of his victims, the press called the unknown offender the Vampire of Düsseldorf.

The crime series was brought to an end when a young woman he had choked and raped but left alive was able to take the police to Kürten's home. Kürten was caught the following day, May 24, 1930, thanks to help from his wife, who had not suspected that her husband was the wanted man. She even received a reward for turning him in.

Kürten was charged with nine cases of murder and thirty-two cases of attempted murder. He confessed to more attacks than that, although several of his stories apparently were made up. Despite pleading to be not guilty by reason of insanity, Kürten was sentenced to death. He was executed by guillotine on July 2, 1931. Before the execution he asked if he would be able to hear, if only for

Investigators and volunteers searched for bodies of Kürten's victims. The madman had lured several of them to the woods, where he terrorized them.

a moment, his own blood gushing out when his head was chopped off, which he considered the ultimate pleasure.

The year before his death Kürten was studied by Karl Berg, professor of forensic medicine, who had followed the case since before Kürten was caught. Berg presented his findings in an essay titled *Der Sadist*, one of the first attempts to understand what can drive a person to commit such crimes, which was later translated into English.[12]

The examination of Kürten's brain found no physical aberrations. Today, his preserved head is on display in the Ripley's Believe It or Not Museum in Wisconsin Dells, Wisconsin. Before that, the head was in the possession of a private collector from Hawaii, although it is unclear when and how it came to the United States.[13]

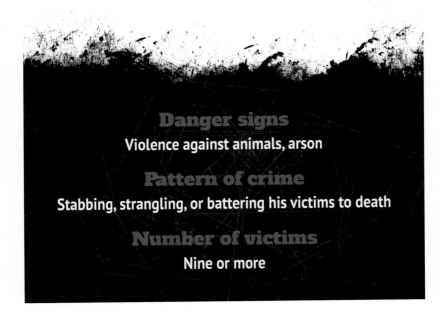

Danger signs

Violence against animals, arson

Pattern of crime

Stabbing, strangling, or battering his victims to death

Number of victims

Nine or more

Ed Gein
aka "The Plainfield Ghoul"

Born: **August 27, 1906**
Profession: **Farmer, Handyman**
Diagnosis: **Schizophrenia**
Arrested: **November 16, 1957**
Died: **July 26, 1984**

A receipt for antifreeze led to the arrest of Edward Theodore Gein in Plainfield, Wisconsin on November 16, 1957. When a local store owner returned from a hunting trip to find a pool of blood on the floor and his mother, who had been manning the store, missing, he became worried. The sales slip reminded him that Ed Gein, an odd character living on a farm at the edge of town, had ordered antifreeze and told him that he would come in to pick it up on this day.

When the police went to investigate at Gein's farm, they found the body of the missing woman, decapitated, hung upside down, and eviscerated. Additionally they discovered ten other female heads and other human remains, some of them turned into decorations or objects of daily use. The heart of Gein's latest victim was found on the stove, which seemed to contradict his later assertion not to have committed any acts of cannibalism. The most bizarre finds, though, were wearable masks and leggings fashioned from human skin, and a vest with breasts.

Ed Gein carved up the bodies of his murder victims. It is believed he consumed some of them. He also made clothing from their skin.

Gein was born on August 27, 1906 as the second son of an alcoholic father and a dominant, puritan mother who tried to keep her sons isolated. Other than going to school they were not allowed to have outside contact, and she spoke out against her sons getting involved with girls in particular because she, a fanatical Lutheran, considered women to be sinful.

The other members of Gein's family died over the span of just a few years: His father died from a heart attack in 1940; his brother was killed in a fire in 1944 (there were suspicions at the time that Gein had killed his brother, but there was no clear evidence); and finally his mother whom he idolized passed away in December 1945 after a series of strokes.

Alone now, Gein stayed on the farm, but he sealed off large parts of the big house, only keeping a small room and a kitchen to live in. He no longer worked the farm, either, as he could live off federal subsidies. But he would suppliment his income by doing odd jobs for the people of Plainfield, who perceived Gein as eccentric but helpful and reasonably friendly.

Soon after the death of his mother, Gein started opening graves in local cemeteries to steal parts of bodies or complete corpses. These he turned into a costume of sorts that he could wear to become a woman, and in this getup he would dance in the moonlight.

Gein had been suspected of another murder, committed on December 8, 1954, but proof that he was the killer was found only three years later after he had been arrested. Gein only confessed to these two murders, claiming that he procured the other human remains discovered in his home by robbing graves. There were

Police investigating Gein's living quarters found a chaotic mess. They also found human costumes and a heart on the stove.

suspicions that he might have claimed more victims, but there was no concrete evidence.

Gein was found unfit for trial and sent to a mental hospital. Eleven years after his arrest the case was finally brought to trial, and Gein was found guilty of murder but legally insane. He was sent back to the hospital, where he died of lung cancer on July 26, 1984.[14]

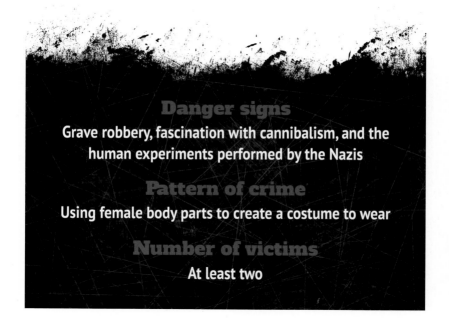

Danger signs

Grave robbery, fascination with cannibalism, and the human experiments performed by the Nazis

Pattern of crime

Using female body parts to create a costume to wear

Number of victims

At least two

Joachim Kroll

Born: April 17, 1933
Profession: Lavatory attendant
Motive: Sadism
Arrested: July 3, 1976
Died: July 1, 1991

The police were searching for a missing four-year-old girl in Duisburg, Germany, when, on July 3, 1976, a local resident complained about one of the shared toilets in his apartment building being backed up. His neighbor, Joachim Kroll, had told him that he had accidentally clogged it with the innards of a rabbit he slaughtered, which aroused suspicions.

It was human entrails that were found in the wastewater pipes. In Kroll's freezer there was human flesh packed in plastic bags, and in a pot on the stove, amidst carrots and potatoes, lay a tiny hand. Kroll confessed that he had had a taste of it but did not find it to his liking.

Kroll was born on April 17, 1933 as the sixth of ten children of a miner in Hindenburg, Upper Silesia (part of Germany at the time, now Zabrze, Poland). He was frequently beaten by his father, but that was not the only violence he experienced; near the end of World War II, when the Soviets were pushing westwards into Germany torn-up corpses were not an uncommon sight. In 1947 the family came to

Joachim Kroll got his start with animals, sexually abusing and eviscerating them, before turning to humans. His hobby of murdering people also provided him with food.

western Germany where Kroll had to work as a farmhand. The boy, who was still wetting the bed at this time, had to leave school in 1948 because he was too old. Due to having to repeat a year twice and the turmoil of the war, he had only made it to the fourth grade. In an intelligence test administered after his arrest, Kroll scored only seventy-eight points.

While working on farms he helped slaughter animals, which he found fascinating and stimulating, and he began to fantasize about eviscerating a human being in a similar manner. He is also known to have sexually abused cows and dogs.[15] His single attempt at a normal sexual relationship with a woman was a failure, and so he turned his attention to partners who could not complain about his performance. In 1955, he claimed his first victim, a nineteen-year-old girl he strangled, raped, and disemboweled. He confessed to have killed at least thirteen more times over the course of the next twenty-one years, although investigators believed that these confessions were only the tip of the iceberg, and Kroll claimed at one point that he might have murdered twenty or even thirty people. It is possible, though, that this self-incrimination was influenced by the way the impressionable man was questioned, and Kroll later repudiated his confessions.

Except for the last time he killed, Kroll usually did not look for victims close to his home. Instead, he traveled to neighboring cities in the densely populated Ruhr Area to find a girl or young woman he would strangle before sexually abusing the body. In some cases he cut pieces of flesh from the victims to cook and eat later, although he claimed that this was not sexually motivated but simply pragmatic as meat was expensive. Kroll's only male victim was killed because the murderer was after the man's fiancée. Kroll had observed the two in their car and lured the man outside to stab him. The woman managed to almost run the attacker over with the car and drive him away. Her description of the killer, an unremarkable little man, yielded no results, though, and he was at large for another eleven years before he was finally caught.[16]

The trial began in 1979, more than three years after his arrest, and lasted for more than two-and-a-half years. In the end Kroll was convicted of murder in eight cases and one attempted murder, resulting in eight consecutive life sentences. He died from a heart attack while in prison on July 1, 1991.

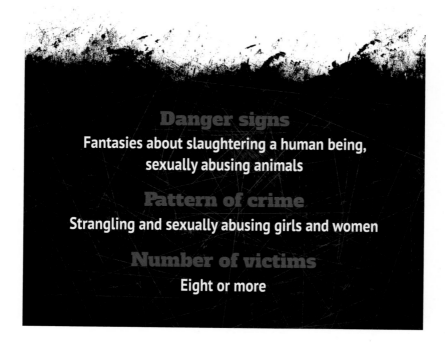

Danger signs

Fantasies about slaughtering a human being, sexually abusing animals

Pattern of crime

Strangling and sexually abusing girls and women

Number of victims

Eight or more

Donald Henry Gaskins

aka "The Meanest Man in America"

Born: March 13, 1933
Profession: Criminal
Motive: Sadism
Arrested: November 14, 1975
Died: September 6, 1991 (executed)

On November 14, 1975, Donald Henry Gaskins returned home to find the police waiting at his house. He was apprehended at the bus station before he could leave the state. Gaskins was sought for contributing to the delinquency of a minor after it had been established that a thirteen-year-old girl who had gone missing had often been seen in his company. It became clear that he had done much more when an accomplice confessed that he had helped Gaskins dispose of several bodies and led the police to their graves in Gaskins's own private graveyard. Gaskins was charged with eight counts of murder, for which he was sentenced to die on May 28, 1976, although this was commuted to eight life sentences in prison later that year. Later confessions revealed that these eight murders were just the tip of the iceberg.

Gaskins was born on March 13, 1933 as Donald Henry Parrot Jr. in Florence County, South Carolina. When he learned that he was the illegitimate son of a wealthy landowner named Gaskins, he adopted

Shackled and handcuffed, Donald "Pee Wee" Gaskins directed Florence County, South Carolina, officers to the area where he'd buried human bones.

that name. He was frequently beaten by his stepfather, and he fought with other children in school on a daily basis.

Gaskins left school at age eleven to work at a garage repairing cars. There he met two other boys with whom he committed burglaries, picked up prostitutes, and raped little boys as well as the sister of one of his partners-in-crime, a deed that led to the trio being broken up.

After seriously wounding a girl who had surprised him during a burglary in 1946, Gaskins was sent to a reform school until he turned eighteen where, due to his small stature that had earned him the nickname Pee Wee, he was frequently the victim of sexual violence.

Shortly after release from the reform school, he was sentenced to six years in prison in 1952 for attacking the daughter of the farmer he was working for with a hammer. Finding himself once again a victim of other inmates' brutality, Gaskins decided to kill another inmate to gain status as a way to protect himself.

After his release in August 1961 he continued his life of crime by breaking into homes again. In 1963 he was sent to prison again for statutory rape. He was paroled in 1968, and the following year his series of murders started when in September 1969 he beat a female hitchhiker unconscious, raped and tortured her, and finally drowned her in a swamp.

Gaskins continued to hunt for victims along the coastal highway of South Carolina, preferably young women and girls. He enjoyed prolonging the suffering of his victims, sometimes raping and torturing them for days and cannibalizing parts of their bodies while they were still alive or forcing them to eat their own flesh. Additionally he started killing people he knew, often other criminals he was working with and who had crossed him or knew too much, but he also acted as a contract killer. Even while in prison he killed a death row inmate for money by rigging a portable radio with explosives in 1982. For this last murder Gaskins was sentenced to death, and he was executed by electric chair on September 6, 1991.[17]

The number of Gaskins's victims is unclear. In his autobiography, posthumously published in 1993, he claimed to have killed more than a hundred people, but former Florence County Sheriff Billy Barnes expressed his doubts that there were more than the thirteen victims he was aware of, believing that Gaskins would have made use of the opportunity to lead the police to the bodies if there had been any more.[18]

Danger signs

History of violence and sexual abuse

Pattern of crime

Varied

Number of victims

Thirteen or more

Andrei Chikatilo
aka "The Rostov Ripper"

Born: October 16, 1936
Profession: Teacher
Motive: Sadism
Arrested: November 20, 1990
Died: February 14, 1994 (executed)

Andrei Chikatilo was born on October 16, 1936 in Yablochnoye, Ukraine (part of the Soviet Union at the time). The great famine that killed millions of Ukrainians in the early 1930s had left its mark on Chikatilo's family; his mother told her children the story that an older brother of theirs, Stepan, was kidnapped and cannibalized during that time. The family was poor and often did not have enough to eat. Chikatilo witnessed the horrors of World War II firsthand, and he wet the bed longer than considered normal. His father had been taken prisoner by the Germans, for which he was sent to a prison camp as a traitor by the Soviets when the war was over, making the family outcasts.

Chikatilo was fearful and insecure growing up, and his low self-esteem took another hit when he discovered that he suffered from impotence. Nonetheless he got married in 1963 and fathered a daughter, born in 1965, and a son, born four years later. After his military service he worked as a telephone engineer near Rostov-on-Don, but he became a teacher in 1971. He was terminated from

Imagine if this man were your teacher. Andrei Chikatilo lured young women and children into secluded areas and stabbed them to death. Because he sometimes mutilated the flesh of his victims with his teeth, he is known as the Rostov Ripper.

this job after sexually assaulting female students. He found another job at a mining school in Shakty, where the family relocated to in 1978.

That year, he committed his first murder. On December 22, he lured a nine-year-old girl into a shack he had bought, blindfolded her, and stabbed her several times before throwing her into the nearby river. Through violence, he achieved the sexual arousal he was otherwise incapable of experiencing. The body was found two days later and Chikatilo, whose history as a child molester was known, was questioned, but the police let him go, instead arresting and executing another man for Chikatilo's crime although he had an alibi.

In 1981, Chikatilo took a new job for a factory that required him to travel. He used this opportunity to hunt for more victims, children and young women, near train and bus stations. He lured them into nearby forest strips and killed them, usually by stabbing them over and over. In some cases he mutilated them with his teeth, devouring parts of their bodies, possibly while his victims were still alive. Because of the brutality of his murders he was nicknamed the Rostov Ripper.

In September 1984, Chikatilo was picked up by the police after he had been observed for nine hours trying to pick up women near Rostov's central bus station. Although he was found to be carrying a long knife, he was ruled out as being the killer because his blood type did not match the semen type found at the crime scenes, a rare anomaly that worked in Chikatilo's favor. Instead, he was sentenced to a year in prison for theft from a previous employer, but he was released after three months.

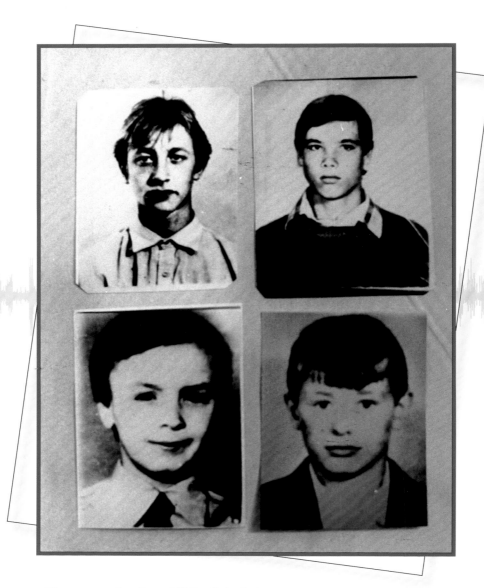

These are only a few of Chikatilo's victims. In all, he is believed to have murdered at least fifty-two women and children.

Despite a massive investigation during which half a million people were interviewed and a remarkably accurate profile of the killer was produced, Chikatilo was not arrested for the murders until November 1990. He had been observed by a policeman emerging from the woods near the train station in Donkleshoz, where a week later the mutilated corpse of a young woman was found. Chikatilo was placed under surveillance, and after he had been observed again trying to pick up women and children, he was arrested on November 20, and it was discovered that the places of the murders coincided with Chikatilo's business trips. Chikatilo confessed to have committed fifty-five murders, while he had been suspected of "only" thirty-six. He was charged with fifty-three murders, and after six months of trial in 1992, during which Chikatilo at one point claimed to have killed even more people, he was found guilty of fifty-two murders and sentenced to die.[19] He was executed on February 14, 1994.

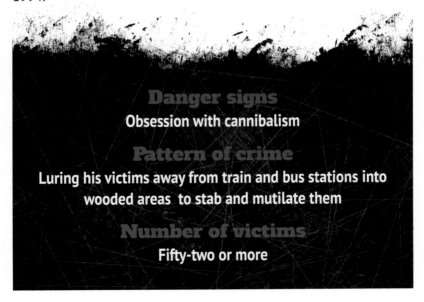

Danger signs
Obsession with cannibalism

Pattern of crime
Luring his victims away from train and bus stations into wooded areas to stab and mutilate them

Number of victims
Fifty-two or more

Ottis Elwood Toole

Born: **March 5, 1947**
Profession: **Criminal**
Motive: **Sadism**
Arrested: **July 1983**
Died: **September 15, 1996**

Toole was born on March 5, 1947 in Jacksonville, Florida, to a Christian extremist mother and an alcoholic father who soon left the family. By his maternal grandmother, whom Toole claimed was a Satanist, he was introduced to grave robbing. His sister reportedly forced him to wear girls clothing and called him Becky. Additionally he was sexually abused by a male friend of his father when he was five years old. Toole became an arsonist, being aroused by fire.

Toole, who had an IQ of seventy-five and suffered from attention deficit/hyperactivity disorder (ADHD) and dyslexia as well as seizures, dropped out of school in ninth grade and started working as a prostitute to finance his drug and alcohol abuse. He killed for the first time when he was fourteen, running over a traveling salesman who wanted to have sex. After drifting around the United States for several years, during which he was arrested numerous times for loitering, theft, and other petty crimes, he returned to Jacksonville in 1975. He had become a suspect in two murders, one in Nebraska, the

Ottis Elwood Toole didn't have much of a chance in life, being the product of an unstable and possibly depraved family. Toole murdered at least six victims as sacrifices in his satanic cult, enjoying the roasted flesh of at least one.

In 1976, Toole met Henry Lee Lucas, who had spent ten years in prison for killing his own mother, at a soup kitchen. They started a sexual relationship and became partners in crime as well. Toole claimed that while they were together, Lucas and he murdered more than 200 people all across the country. Allegedly they were influenced by a satanic cult that ritually sacrificed humans who were then cannibalized. Toole and Lucas kidnapped children and women for the cult and acted as hitmen after receiving training in the Florida Everglades. Toole also claimed to have roasted and eaten people he killed for sexual purposes. Bizarrely, he even made his own barbeque sauce to enjoy them with.[20] That Lucas did not partake was not due to his aversion of eating human flesh, but his dislike of barbeque sauce in general and Toole's recipe in particular.

Toole was arrested in July 1983 for arson and sentenced to twenty years in prison. While behind bars, he confessed to several murders, including the abduction and decapitation of Adam Walsh in 1981. Adam was the son of John Walsh, who went on to become an anticrime activist, hosting *America's Most Wanted*. Toole later recanted this confession and many others. He was found guilty of locking a man in his house and setting it on fire in January 1982, and of strangling a young woman in February 1983. For these crimes he received two death penalties that were commuted to two life sentences. After he pled guilty to four more murders in 1991, another four years were added to his sentence. Toole died in prison of cirrhosis on September 15, 1996.

Henry Lee Lucas was arrested in June 1983 on weapons charges. Both men made incredible claims concerning their crimes. If true, their rampage would be unparalleled, but many of the

In 2008, authorities finally confirmed that Ottis Elwood Toole had murdered six-year-old Adam Walsh. His family (left to right: sister Meghan, mother Reve, brother Hayden, father John, and brother Callahan) gathered to attend a press conference.

confessions are believed to have been false so that the full extent of their crimes is unknown. More than ten years after Toole's death, though, the Hollywood, Florida, police department confirmed in 2008 that he was indeed the murderer of Adam Walsh. Investigators had reexamined the circumstantial evidence collected over the years and concluded that it all pointed to Toole. Finally, Walsh's family had a small but important measure of closure.

Danger signs

Setting fires

Pattern of crime

Varied

Number of victims

Six or more

Edmund Kemper
aka "The Co-ed Killer"

Born: **December 18, 1948**
Profession: **Laborer for the State Highway Department**
Motive: **Hatred for his mother, sadism**
Arrested: **April 22, 1973**

Edmund Emil Kemper III was born on December 18, 1948 as the second of three children. His parents separated when Kemper was seven, and he blamed the absence of his father on his mother, who was overly strict in the attempt to make up for a male presence and frequently criticized and humiliated him. When he was eight years old, his mother told young Edmund that he was to sleep in the basement from then on because he made his sisters feel uncomfortable. Kemper was exceptionally large even at that age and would grow up to be a massive 6' 9" (approximately two meters), weighing around 300 pounds (136 kilograms). Until his father finally protested, Kemper was banished to this dark and scary room that was only accessible through a trapdoor under a table.

Kemper's younger sister recalled strange behavior on his part, even at an early age. He liked to play execution, acting out his own death. His fascination with violence and death also was apparent when he cut off the head and hands of his sister's doll. These fantasies soon extended to humans as Kemper harbored thoughts

Edmund Kemper was escorted to court on April 25, 1973. This man who had been obsessed with violence and death as a child killed his grandparents and mother, along with six young women and girls.

about killing his mother, as well as a teacher and neighbors (and also to have sex with their dead bodies). By age thirteen he was killing animals, sometimes putting the severed heads of cats on spikes as trophies.

Since his mother did not know how to handle him, Kemper was sent to live with his paternal grandparents at their ranch in northern California. Kemper resented this, and when he was fifteen he killed his grandparents, first shooting and stabbing his grandmother while he was alone with her at the house, then shooting his grandfather when he returned. He was sent to a mental hospital, but he was released when he was twenty-one and sent back to his mother, with whom he continued to struggle because she verbally abused him.

In May 1972 he began a series of murders that claimed the lives of six girls and young women, mainly hitchhiking college students. After stabbing, strangling, or shooting his victims, he would decapitate them and have sex with the bodies before dismembering them, keeping some flesh in two cases to eat later, and then disposing of the rest. The heads he kept longer than the bodies as trophies and for sexual gratification. He boldly frequented police bars to talk to the officers about the so-called Co-ed Killer, without being suspected of anything.

On April 21, 1973, Kemper beat his mother to death with a hammer before decapitating her, sexually abusing the corpse, and using the head as a dartboard. Later that day he invited his mother's best friend over for dinner, only to strangle and decapitate her as well. The next day he left home, driving eastwards, waiting for reports of the murders to come on the radio. When there were none, he stopped in Pueblo, Colorado, to call the Santa Cruz police.

Aiko Koo was one of Kemper's young victims. Koo was hitchhiking because she had missed her bus to dance class. Kemper was more than happy to help the fifteen-year-old, offering her a ride before holding her at gunpoint and strangling her to death.

It took several attempts before the police took him seriously, and finally he was taken into custody and returned to Santa Cruz, where he confessed his crimes.

Kemper pleaded not guilty by reason of insanity, but he was found to be legally sane and, although he asked for the death penalty, he was sentenced to life imprisonment in November 1973.[21]

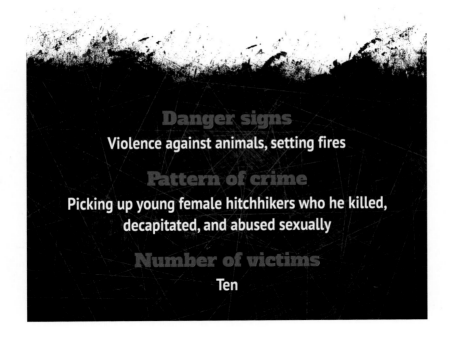

Danger signs
Violence against animals, setting fires

Pattern of crime
Picking up young female hitchhikers who he killed, decapitated, and abused sexually

Number of victims
Ten

Nikolai Dzhumagaliev
aka "The Metal Fang"

Born: **1952**

Profession: **Firefighter**

Motive: **Sadism**

Arrested: **1980, March 1995**

Dzhumagaliev (alternatively transcribed from Cyrillic as Dzhurmongaliev) was born in 1952 in Kazakhstan. Little is known about his childhood other than that he had three siblings. Dzhumagaliev served in the army and worked as a firefighter.

As far as is known, he claimed his first victim in 1978, a twenty-six-year-old woman from a neighboring village. Dzhumagaliev raped and killed his victims, attractive young women, with a knife or an axe which he carried in a backpack, before cutting up the bodies. As an avid hunter he had a good understanding of anatomy. The remains he disposed of methodically, going so far as to crush the teeth of his victims, which he knew would not be destroyed by fire, so that the victims would be impossible to identify. He collected the blood to drink and parts of the flesh for eating. He not only ate the flesh himself, he allegedly invited unwitting guests to join him in the consumption of his victims.

He was caught in 1980, when the decapitated body of a young woman was found in his parents' house. Dzhumagaliev was convicted of committing seven murders but found not guilty by reason of insanity and sent to a mental hospital. He managed to escape in 1989

Nikolai Dzhumagaliev's (second from left) artificial metal teeth only made stories about his cannibalistic killing more chilling. After murdering his victims, he liked to carve up their bodies and consume their flesh and blood.

Authorities tracked and captured Dzhumagaliev after he escaped from a Russian mental hospital in 1989.

while being transported to another facility. He was captured again two years later in Fergana in Uzbekistan. During the time he was missing he spent several months in Moscow, and an investigator working the case believed that he might have killed two women per week in that period.

He was released from a mental institution in Uzbekistan in 1994, because local authorities thought that Dzhumagaliev's native Kazakhstan should take care of him. In March 1995 he was arrested again in Kyrgysztan when he was found drunkenly climbing the fence of a government building. He was returned to the mental institution, from which he granted an interview in the mid-2000s. Dzhumagaliev is sometimes called the Metal Fang, because he had some missing teeth replaced with ones made from metal.

How many victims Dzhumagaliev claimed remains a mystery, although some estimate he might have killed 100 women or more. He rationalized his murders by claiming that he did society a favor by getting rid of prostitutes in his fight against matriarchy.[22]

Danger signs
Unknown

Pattern of crime
Raping and killing young women with a knife or an axe

Number of victims
Seven or more

Dorangel Vargas
aka "El Comagente"

Born: **1957**

Diagnosis: **Paranoid schizophrenia**

Arrested: **February 1999**

Throughout 1998 many people had gone missing near the Libertador Bridge in San Cristobal, Venezuela. The homeless use the bridge as shelter, and one of them, Dorangel (sometimes spelled Dorancel) Vargas, was arrested in February 1999. Human remains were found in his shack, and Vargas readily confessed to have eaten the missing parts, claiming hunger as his motivation. Enough body parts were discovered to confirm that there had been at least twelve victims. Vargas gave detailed accounts of his preparation of the flesh, which gained a lot of attention in the Venezuelan media, who dubbed the cannibal the Hannibal Lecter of the Andes. Vargas, who likened eating human flesh to eating pears, hunted lean men between thirty and forty years of age; he considered women and children too innocent to consume.

Vargas, who was born in 1957, had already been taken into custody once before for killing and eating a man. Since he was found to be mentally ill he could not be held in jail, and he was released in 1995. Vargas claims to be haunted by spirits, and he

Homeless and hungry, Dorangel Vargas killed passersby and ate them for dinner. Once caught and arrested in 1999, Vargas was kept in this holding cell. He remains in custody there today because he cannot legally be thrown in prison.

has been diagnosed with paranoid schizophrenia. He remains in a legal limbo because the mentally ill cannot be sent to prison, but there is no facility for the criminally insane in Venezuela. As a result, Vargas has been kept in a cell by the police of San Cristobal since his arrest to prevent him from harming anyone else.[23]

Danger signs
Unknown

Pattern of crime
Hunting men between thirty and forty years of age to eat

Number of victims
Thirteen or more

Jeffrey Dahmer
aka "The Milwaukee Cannibal"

Born: **May 21, 1960**
Profession: **Worker at a chocolate factory**
Motive: **Sadism**
Arrested: **July 22, 1991**
Died: **November 28, 1994 (killed by
a fellow inmate)**

On May 27, 1991, three policemen who had been called by a concerned resident found a boy wandering the streets. He was naked and bleeding, and he seemed completely disoriented. A man appeared and told officers the boy was staying with him and had had too much to drink. The officers escorted them back to the man's apartment, where everything seemed to be in order. The man was Jeffrey Dahmer, and if the policemen had bothered to check they would have found a corpse in his bedroom. They also could have saved the life of the boy they entrusted in his care, as well as the lives of four more victims Dahmer claimed before he finally was caught.

Only two months later, on July 22, 1991, Dahmer was arrested when one of his victims managed to flee from his apartment despite being drugged and handcuffed. He ran into some police officers and told them that he had been threatened with a knife. When the officers went to investigate Dahmer's home, they found photographs

The discovery and reporting of Jeffrey Dahmer's cannibalism shook Americans to the core. Dahmer routinely picked up men for sex, murdered them, and eviscerated their bodies.

of mutilated bodies, several human skulls, and severed heads in his bedroom.

Dahmer was born in 1960 to a middle-class family, followed by a younger brother six years later. When he was in first grade, a teacher noted that Dahmer felt neglected. His parents' relationship was not harmonious, but they decided to stay together for the sake of their children and only got a divorce when Dahmer was eighteen. Stories that he was sexually abused as a child by a neighbor were denied by Dahmer, and there does not seem to be anything particularly out of the ordinary concerning his childhood. Yet he was fascinated by dead bodies from an early age, curious to see what bodies looked like from the inside and how they worked. To this end he collected the carcasses of animals that had been run over, and he killed animals like cats and dogs, putting their heads on spikes. At age fourteen, Dahmer, a loner perceived by his schoolmates as weird and emotionless, was fantasizing about having sex with a dead body. He also developed a drinking problem.

In 1978, Dahmer killed a human for the first time, an eighteen-year-old hitchhiker. After picking him up and inviting him to his house, Dahmer killed him to prevent him from leaving. He then dismembered the body and scattered the remains.

Dahmer dropped out of college after just one term, and then spent two years in the US Army but was discharged because of his alcohol abuse. This proved too much to handle for his father and stepmother, so Dahmer was sent to live with his grandmother in the hopes that she would have a positive influence on him. This seemed to work at first, even though Dahmer was arrested for indecent exposure a couple of times.

In 1987, Dahmer began murdering. His victims were boys and young men, most of them black, who he picked up for sex. According to a young woman Dahmer befriended in 1988, he spoke out against homosexuals, apparently deeply conflicted about his own sexuality. He would sedate his victims with sleeping pills mixed into a beverage, kill them, and abuse their bodies before dismembering them and disposing of the parts. Dahmer had already claimed three victims by the summer of 1988, when his unsuspecting grandmother asked him to move out.

He lured a thirteen-year-old Laotian boy to his own Milwaukee apartment and drugged him. This encounter led to Dahmer's arrest for sexual assault and sexual exploitation. But while he was out on bail, awaiting sentencing, Dahmer killed another man. This time he kept the severed head. The court sent Dahmer to a correction center for a year for his sexual assault on the teenage boy, completely in the dark about his other crimes.

After his release, Dahmer killed twelve more times following the same routine before getting arrested in July 1991. He kept parts of his victims, usually the genitals and the skulls, the full skeleton in one case. He confessed to eating the flesh of some of his victims, and he conducted experiments on some of them while they were still alive, drilling holes into their skulls and injecting acid into their brains, apparently in an attempt to lobotomize them and turn them into mindless sex slaves.

Dahmer confessed to seventeen murders, but he was only charged with fifteen because for one case there was a lack of evidence, and for his first murder, committed in Ohio, he was to stand trial separately. On February 15, 1992, Dahmer was declared sane and sent to prison for fifteen consecutive life sentences,

Milwaukee police load Dahmer's refrigerator into a truck. Once Dahmer was discovered, authorities investigated his home, where they found grisly evidence of Dahmer's activities, including body parts stored inside the refrigerator.

followed by a sixteenth life sentence a few months later. Due to his celebrity, Dahmer was placed in solitary confinement for his own personal safety for the first year of his imprisonment. He became a born-again Christian and claimed he was ready to die when fellow prisoners made attempts on his life. On November 28, 1994, while on work detail, Dahmer was bludgeoned to death by two inmates.[24]

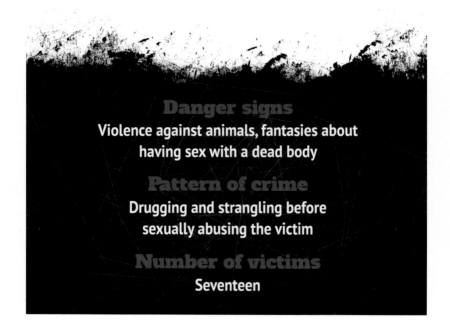

Danger signs

Violence against animals, fantasies about having sex with a dead body

Pattern of crime

Drugging and strangling before sexually abusing the victim

Number of victims

Seventeen

Tsutomu Miyazaki

aka "The Otaku Murderer"

Born: **August 21, 1962**
Profession: **Photo technician**
Motive: **Sadism**
Arrested: **July 23, 1989**
Died: **June 17, 2008 (executed)**

On July 23, 1989, Tsutomu Miyazaki was arrested after molesting and trying to take photos of a little girl in a park. At first he was able to flee on foot after being confronted by the girl's father, but the police caught him when he returned to retrieve his car. It soon became clear that he was the serial killer the police had been trying to find for almost a year. In his home remains were found of his victims, all young girls, as well as a huge collection of nearly 6,000 videotapes with anime, porn, and horror movies, which were suspected to have fueled his violent fantasies. This collection earned him the nickname "Otaku Murderer," *otaku* being the Japanese term for an obsessive fan of anime and manga, bringing a whole subculture into disrepute.

Miyazaki was born on August 21, 1962 in Itsukaichi, Tokyo, Japan to a wealthy and influential family. He was teased mercilessly because his hands were deformed and incapable of turning at the wrist. Miyazaki, who did not feel accepted by his family and was unable to find any friends, became a loner, withdrawing into his own

Tsutomu Miyazaki felt disenfranchised from childhood, a loner living in a violent fantasy world. He claimed his murders were committed by an alter ego called Rat Man. In spite of his mental issues, Miyazaki was found accountable for his crimes and sentenced to death.

fantasy world. His plans to go to university to become a teacher fell through due to poor grades, and he instead settled for a future as a photo technician.

In May 1988, Miyazaki's grandfather, the only member of his family he had felt close to, died. He later claimed to have consumed some of the ashes of his grandfather's cremated bones.

Three months later, Miyazaki abducted and strangled his first victim, a four-year-old girl. Over the following months he killed three more times, little girls between four and seven years of age. He engaged in sexual acts with the corpses, and he drank the blood and ate parts of his last victim. Additionally, he terrorized the parents of his victims by sending them postcards with cryptic messages alluding to their daughters' fate. In one case he placed the remains of a girl on her parents' doorstep in a cardboard box, followed by a detailed letter. Despite these hints and a massive investigation, the police were unable to identify the murderer before he was caught by chance and confessed.

According to one psychologist, Miyazaki believed that his murders would resurrect his grandfather, while others found he suffered from a multiple personality disorder or schizophrenia. In fact, Miyazaki claimed that it was an alter ego called "Rat Man" that forced him to commit his crimes. Nonetheless the court found that he was aware of the gravity of his crimes and therefore accountable, and Miyazaki was sentenced to death in 1997. After the sentence had been upheld twice, Miyazaki finally was hanged on June 17, 2008 without ever having expressed any remorse for his murders. His father, unable to cope with what his son had done, committed suicide in 1994 by jumping into a river.[25]

Danger signs

Violent fantasies

Pattern of crime

Abducting, strangling, and sexually abusing little girls

Number of victims

Four

Yoo Young-chul

Born: 1970
Profession: Criminal
Motive: Hatred of rich people, sadism
Arrested: July 15, 2004

Yoo Young-chul was arrested on July 15, 2004 on suspicion of assault on a masseuse, but he was able to escape after faking a seizure. He was caught again the next day and confessed to killing twenty-one people, making him the serial killer with the most victims in the history of South Korea.

Yoo was born in 1970 as the fourth child of a poor family. He experienced physical abuse and often went hungry. Prior to his arrest in 2004 he had already spent a total of eleven years in prison for fourteen different counts of theft, forgery, robbery, and rape.

After his prison term for raping a fifteen-year-old girl was over in September 2003, he turned to murder. First he chose wealthy people as his victims, breaking into houses in and around Seoul during the day when only older family members were likely to be home, and killing the people he encountered with a hammer. He did not steal anything from the houses he broke into, which shows that his motive was not greed but hatred of the rich and a social system he perceived

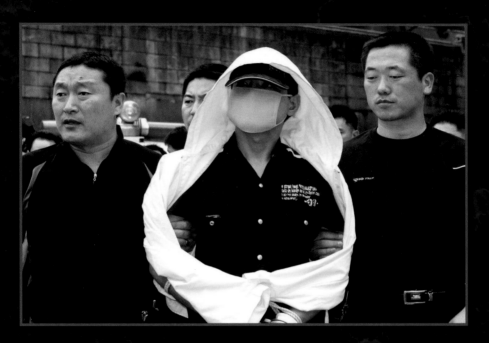

After confessing to murdering more than twenty people, Yoo Young-chul was escorted by authorities to sites in Seoul, Korea, where he claimed to have buried the bodies of his victims. Yoo had an irrational hatred of the rich, and he set upon murdering them to rally against a social system he believed was unfair.

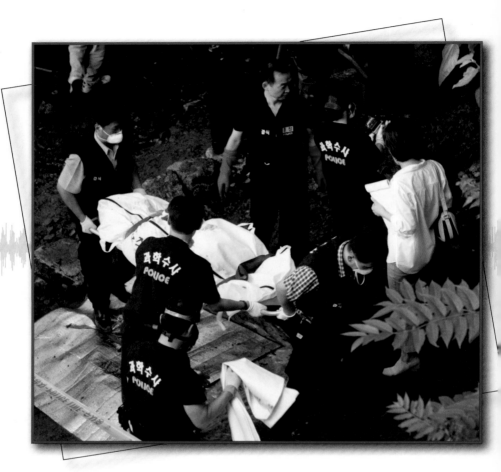

Police officials remove the body of one of Yoo's victims from an investigation scene in Seoul. Along with the wealthy, Yoo targeted prostitutes in an attempt to avenge the rejections he had experienced from women in the past.

In 2004, he began to target prostitutes, possibly motivated by the fact that an escort girl turned down his advances, fueling his hatred of women. He later told the police that he considered killing his wife after she divorced him in 2002 while he was in prison, but refrained from doing so out of respect for his son. Instead he called escort services to send girls to his apartment, where he killed them with a hammer, before dismembering them and burying the remains near a Buddhist temple. He confessed to eating the livers of some of his victims, and he said that he would have continued killing until he claimed a hundred victims if he had not been caught.

Yoo was sentenced to death on June 19, 2005, although the death penalty had not been carried out in South Korea for eight years. This led to a debate on capital punishment, and Yoo himself spoke out against abolishing the death penalty, stating that it would be unfair to let people like him live.[26]

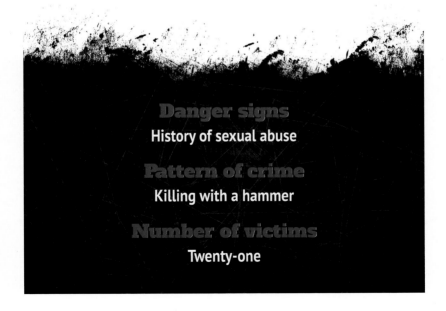

Danger signs
History of sexual abuse

Pattern of crime
Killing with a hammer

Number of victims
Twenty-one

Alexander Spesivtsev
aka "The Siberian Tiger"

Born: **March 1, 1970**
Profession: **Unemployed**
Motive: **Sadism**
Arrested: **October 27, 1996**

Neighbors complained about the smell emanating from the apartment of Alexander Spesivtsev in Novokusnetsk, an industrial town in Siberia, in the summer of 1996, but the police refused to do anything about it. It took another four months before they came to break down Spesivtsev's door because he refused to open up to let the plumber in to check the pipes on October 24, 1996. Spesivtsev fled by jumping from the window to the roof of another building. The police found the apartment covered in blood and filled with severed body parts. But they also saw that Spesivtsev's last victim was still alive, despite being stabbed in the abdomen. The fifteen-year-old girl was able to tell them that an old lady had lured her and two of her friends to the apartment, where they were attacked by Spesivtsev. He had stabbed one of the girls and forced the other two to dismember her body and eat a soup made from the remains. The torture lasted for a month, and the last remaining of the three girls died from her injuries the day after being freed. Spesivtsev was caught three days later when he returned to his neighborhood.

Alexander Spesivtsev, also called Sasha or Sanya, was born on March 1, 1970, a small and sickly child. His father was a violent alcoholic, and his mother, Lyudmila, slept in the same bed as her son as a defense against her husband. Lyudmila kept up this practice until Spesivtsev was twelve years old, even though she had left her husband seven years earlier. Growing up, Spesivtsev committed petty crimes like theft and vandalism, and he enjoyed reading the material about criminal cases his mother brought home from her work as a lawyer's assistant, including pictures of corpses. He was hospitalized because of mental health issues when he was eighteen. After his release he married a seventeen-year-old girl he abused violently, even beating her up in the hospital where she sought treatment for the injuries he inflicted upon her. His young wife died in 1991, and Spesivtsev was committed to a psychiatric clinic, where he was diagnosed with schizophrenia.

After his release in 1995 he began his series of murders. He found his victims, mostly girls and young women, but also some boys, among the poor living in the streets of his hometown. He lured them to his apartment where he bound, raped, tortured, and killed them. Sometimes his mother helped out, approaching young people on the streets and delivering them to her son. She also disposed of the victims' remains by throwing them in the river. And she cooked parts of their flesh for her son to eat. In 1996, police determined that there was a serial killer in their midst when body parts were discovered in the river. Finally, they took the complaints of Spesivtsev's neighbors seriously and investigated his apartment.

Spesivtsev confessed to nineteen murders, although the amount of blood-covered clothes found in his apartment suggests that there might have been more than eighty victims. It is possible, though, that the clothes were acquired in a different way and sprayed with blood when Spesivtsev butchered his victims, so it is unclear how many lives he claimed.

Spesivtsev was sent to a mental institution, while his mother was sentenced to fifteen years in prison for acting as her son's accomplice.[27]

Danger signs

History of violence, fascination with murder

Pattern of crime

Luring victims into his apartment to rape and torture

Number of victims

Nineteen or more

Chapter 4

UNDERSTANDING CANNIBALISTIC SERIAL KILLERS

Consistent with the Holmes typology, most cannibal serial killers appear to be sexually motivated. Some may claim other motivations, but their actions speak louder than words. For example, Nikolai Dzhumagaliev's and Alexander Spesivtsev's assertion to rid society of undesirables seems to be pleaded as an excuse. A killer whose only goal is to fulfill his mission of killing people he considers to be bad has no reason to sexually abuse and consume parts of his victims. Yoo Young-chul seems to have started out as a mission killer when he targeted older rich people, but when he started to claim prostitutes as his victims who he also cannibalized, the sexual motivation clearly became prevalent.

Similarly, citing hunger as a motivation of cannibalistic acts committed by serial killers is an insufficient explanation. If it just

Cannibal Serial Killers

was meat they were after, it defies logic that killers like Karl Denke and Joachim Kroll would go after human victims when stealing farm animals presents a lower risk and, in case of conviction, lesser punishment.

The only clear exceptions are Enriqueta Martí and Leonarda Cianciulli who, like most female serial killers, fall into the category of comfort killers whose motivation is material gain, paired in these cases with a belief in the magical properties of cannibalism. The case of the third female cannibal, Erzsébet (Elizabeth) Báthory, is remarkable precisely because it falls so well in line with the male lust killers. Sadism of this kind is very rare in women, "perhaps because the sense of inadequacy, low self-esteem, powerlessness and frustration which manifests as aggression to others in male sadistic killers is often turned inwards in women, resulting in such things as self-mutilation and suicide."[1] It is not unheard of, though, and according to Hannah Scott's research on female serial killers, 4.9 percent of them used torture as a method of killing, and those women who tortured their victims were all in a position of power over others, just like the Blood Countess.[2] Maybe it is just the lack of opportunity that prevents more female serial killers from bringing their sadism to bear.

Another exception is Dorangel Vargas, who can be classified as a psychotic visionary killer. He was not the only one who claimed to hear voices, though. Albert Fish asserted that he was doing God's will, but while he was found to have a psychopathic personality, he was not considered insane by the psychologists consulted during his trial.[3]

124

Most serial killers do not fit neatly into one category or another. Albert Fish believed he was following God's instructions when he murdered, but he was considered sane by authorities.

Psychosis and Psychopathy

Psychosis and psychopathy are two different mental disorders that are not to be confused. Psychotics have lost contact with reality, they suffer from delusions or hallucinations, which is not the case with psychopaths. Psychopathy or antisocial personality disorder is characterized by calculating, exploitive, and impulsive behavior as well as selfishness, remorselessness, and a lack of empathy, but also by a superficial charm psychopaths can employ to reach their goals. Colloquially, "psychopath" and "serial killer" are sometimes used as synonyms, but they are not. Not all psychopaths become criminals, and not all serial killers are psychopaths, although many show traits associated with psychopathy. It has been suggested that an ordinary type of psychopath who shows antisocial, selfish, and impulsive but not predatory behavior should be distinguished from a malignant type of psychopath "whose goal is the gratification of vengeful or sexual sadistic fantasies."[4]

"Psychopaths who commit serial murder do not value human life and are extremely callous in their interactions with their victims. This is particularly evident in sexually motivated serial killers who repeatedly target, stalk, assault, and kill without a sense of remorse."[5] The inability to feel guilt or remorse is obvious in many, if not all, cannibal serial killers.

The causes of psychopathy are unclear. A study conducted by the University of Minnesota about twins that were reared apart has shown that psychopathy is sixty percent heritable, so genetics play a more important part in who becomes a psychopath than environmental factors (e.g., one's upbringing). It is possible, though, that abuse or neglect suffered in childhood plays a part in a psychopath developing into a violent person.[6]

Warning Signs

There are behavioral characteristics, known as the Macdonald Triad, that are seen as common warning signs that a child might grow up to be violent. These warning signs are named after forensic psychiatrist John Marshall Macdonald, who first described this set of three behaviors and their connection to violence and sadism in an article published in 1963. The Macdonald Triad are: bed-wetting past the age when most children stay dry at night (around the age of six or seven for the vast majority); fascination with setting fires; and cruelty to animals. As the examples in this book show, these behaviors are frequently found in the biographies of serial killers. Of course not every child who has an "accident" in their sleep or who pulls the wings from a fly will become a serial killer, but if two or all three symptoms occur concurrently and repeatedly, that is a strong sign of psychological trauma that needs to be treated professionally. Many serial killers witnessed or were themselves victims of verbal, physical, or sexual abuse in their childhood, which leaves marks on the psyche.

Bed-wetting happens unintentionally and can lead to more emotional stress when the child is punished or ridiculed for it. Committing arson and hurting animals, on the other hand, are active attempts at releasing aggression. Setting fires can be accompanied by fantasies about people coming to harm and possible sexual arousal. Cruelty to animals is seen as the strongest indicator, at least if it is higher animals rather than worms and insects that are the chosen victims. Similar to humans, cats, dogs, and birds feel pain and show fear, they bleed and die, which makes them good substitutes for the person a child actually wants to hurt.[7]

Jeffrey Dahmer exhibited several of the textbook serial killer warning signs, such as bed-wetting, arson, and cruelty to animals. His difficult childhood did not help matters.

Despite its prominence in criminology, the Macdonald Triad is controversial. Critics warn about using it for predicting future violence, stressing that it is not a behavioral syndrome but rather an indicator of experienced abuse.[8] And while many serial killers were victims of child abuse, not all abuse victims grow up to be violent offenders. Looking at the cases presented in this book, many of the killers had siblings who grew up in the same circumstances, but although some ended up having trouble with the law, none of them went down the same path of extreme violence.

The debate of nature versus nurture, the question whether a serial killer is born or made, has not found an answer yet, and quite possibly it is the wrong question to ask. Both genes and outside factors seem to play a part, although the exact reasons why an individual with the genetic disposition turns into a violent killer while another does not are unclear, and finding them will be difficult. Serial murder is a rare phenomenon, less than one percent of the murders committed per year are the work of a serial killer.[9] Serial murder in combination with cannibalism is rarer still, an absolute exception. While these cases usually get a lot of attention in the media because they are so exceptional, their rarity means that we know relatively little about the reasons why a person would become a cannibal killer. And looking at the existing cases, oftentimes it seems that doing away with the offenders who are considered to be beasts and monsters seemed to be a higher priority than to study them thoroughly, which might have helped to understand their development and motivation better. And that understanding could be invaluable for catching future cannibalistic serial killers, or preventing people in danger of such a development from going down that path in the first place by providing the help they need before anybody comes to harm.

Psychopathy Quiz

Are You a Psychopath?

This quiz is designed to help give you some insight into people with psychopathic tendencies. While the quiz is not meant to diagnose psychopathy, it may also give you an idea about whether or not *you* have such tendencies.

Read each of the following statements and answer each honestly. Give yourself two points if the statement definitely describes you, one point if it somewhat describes you, and zero points if it doesn't describe you at all. Tally up the points to see where *you* sit on the psychopathy scale!

1. I'd rather be spontaneous than make plans.
2. I wouldn't have a problem cheating on a boyfriend or girlfriend if I knew I could get away with it.
3. I don't mind ditching plans to hang out with my friends if something better comes along—like a chance to go out with that hot new guy or girl.
4. Seeing animals injured or in pain doesn't bother me.
5. I love excitement and danger.
6. I think it's OK to manipulate others so that I can get ahead.
7. I'm a smooth talker: I can always get people to do what I want them to do.
8. I'm great at making quick decisions.
9. I don't get it when movies or TV shows make people cry.
10. Most people just bring problems upon themselves, so why should I help them?

11. I'm rarely to blame when things go wrong—it's others who are incompetent, not me.
12. I have more talent in the tip of my little finger than most people will ever have.
13. I am able to make other people believe my lies.
14. I don't feel guilty when I make people feel bad.
15. I often borrow things and then lose or forget to return them.
16. I skip school or work more than most people I know.
17. I tend to blurt out exactly what's on my mind.
18. I often get into trouble because I lie a lot.
19. I skip school and/or often don't get my assignments done on time.
20. I think that crying is a sign of weakness.

If you scored 30–40 points, you have many psychopath tendencies.

If you scored 20–39 points, you have some psychopathic tendencies.

If you scored 0–19 points, you have no psychopathic tendencies.

Chapter Notes

Chapter 1: A History of Cannibalism

1. Heidi Peter-Röcher, *Mythos Menschenfresser: Ein Blick in die Kochtöpfe der Kannibalen* (Munich, Germany: Verlag C.H. Beck, 1998), pp. 10–11.
2. "Cannibalism," *Merriam-Webster Dictionary*, http://www.merriam-webster.com/dictionary/cannibal.
3. Manfred Risse, *Abendmahl der Mörder: Kannibalen–Mythos und Wirklichkeit* (Leipizig, Germany: Militzke Verlag, 2007), pp. 19–23.
4. Peter-Röcher, pp. 25–27.
5. Ibid., pp. 68–77.
6. Ibid., p. 76.
7. David Livingstone and Charles Livingstone, *Narrative of an Expedition to the Zambesi and its Tributaries; and of the Discovery of the Lakes Shirwa and Nyassa, 1858–1864* (New York: Harper & Brother, Publishers, 1806), p. 77.
8. Peter-Röcher, pp. 108–109.
9. Risse, pp. 26–27.
10. Maria Dolan, "The Gruesome History of Eating Corpses as Medicine," Smithsonianmag.com, 2012, http://www.smithsonianmag.com/history/the-gruesome-history-of-eating-corpses-as-medicine-82360284/.

Chapter 2: Serial Murder and Cannibalism

1. Robert J. Morton, ed., *Serial Murder: Multi-Disciplinary Perspectives for Investigators*, hhtp://www.fbi.gov/stats-services/publications/serial-murder/serial-murder-july-2008-pdf, p. 9.
2. Ibid., pp. 2–6.
3. Ibid., p. 3.
4. Ronald M. Holmes and Stephen T. Holmes, *Serial Murder*, 3rd ed. (Thousand Oaks, CA: SAGE Publications, 2010), p. 49.

5. Hannah Scott, "The 'Gentler Sex': Patterns in Female Serial Murder, in Richard N. Kocsis, ed., *Serial Murder and the Psychology of Violent Crimes* (Totowa, NJ: Humana Press, 2008), pp. 179–186.
6. Morton, p. 5.
7. Ibid., p. 6.
8. Ibid.
9. Holmes and Holmes, pp. 55–56.
10. Morton, p. 11.
11. Holmes and Holmes, p. 45.

Chapter 3: Examples of Cannibal Serial Killers

1. John J. Eddleston, *Jack the Ripper: An Encyclopedia* (Santa Barbara, CA: ABC, 2001), p. 161.
2. Norbert Borrmann, *Vampirismus oder die Sehnsucht nach Unsterblichkeit* (Kreuzlingen/Munich, Germany: Heinrich Hugendubel Verlag, 1999), pp. 207–211.
3. Tony Thorne, "Countess Elizabeth Báthory: Icon of Evil," *The Telegraph*, 2008, http://www.telegraph.co.uk/culture/ film/3555482/Countess-Elizabeth-Bathory-icon-of-evil.html.
4. Armin Rütters, "Vater Denke" – "Ich Rieche, Rieche Menschenfleich," in Michael Kirchschlager, ed., *Historische Serienmörder II: Menschliche Ungeheuer vom späten Mittelalter bis zur Mitte des 20. Jahrhunderts* (Arnstadt, Germany: Verlag Kirchschlager, 2009), pp. 147–214.
5. Pedro Costa, "La Vampira del Carrer Ponent," *El Pais*, 2006, http:// elpais.com/diario/2006/01/01/eps/1136100421_850215.html.
6. Moira Martingale, *Cannibal Killers: The History of Impossible Murderers* (New York: St. Martin's Press, 1995), pp. 41–55.
7. "OMICIDI: Caso Cianciulli," Museo Criminological, http://www. museocriminologico.it/index.php/2-non-categorizzato/119- omicidi-caso-cianciulli.

8. Theodor Lessing, *Haarmann: Die Geschichte eines Werwolfs* (Berlin, Germany: Rogner & Bernhard, 1973), Chapter 3, http://gutenberg.spiegel.de/buch/haarmann-7706/3.

9. Borrmann, p. 119.

10. Lessing, Chapter 4, http://gutenberg.spiegel.de/buch/haarmann-7706/4.

11. Petra Klages, *Serienmord und Kannibalismus in Deutschland: Fallstudien, Psychologie, Profiling* (Graz, Austria: V.F. Sammler, 2011), pp. 59–103.

12. Katherine Ramsland, *The Mind of a Murderer: Privileged Access to the Demons that Drive Extreme Violence* (Santa Barbara, CA: Praeger, 2011), pp. 17–30.

13. Martin Rath, "Kürtens Kopf," Legal Tribune Online, 2014, http://www.lto.de/recht/feuilleton/f/peter-kuerten-serienmoerder-hinrichtung-rechtsgeschichte/2/.

14. Anil Aggrawal, *Necrophilia: Forensic and Medico-legal Aspects* (Boca Raton, FL: CRC Press, 2011), pp. 133–137.

15. Klages, pp. 30–33.

16. Martingale, pp. 58–65.

17. "Donald 'Pee Wee' Gaskins," Crime Museum, http://www.crimemuseum.org/crime-library/donald-pee-wee-gaskins.

18. "SC's Worst Killer Remembered on Anniversary of His Execution," Carolinalive.com, http://www.carolinalive.com/news/story.aspx?id=660119.

19. Martingale, pp. 152–177.

20. Donald Jacobs and Ashleigh Portales, *Sexual Forensics: Lust, Passion, and Psychopathic Killers* (Santa Barbara, CA: Praeger, 2014), pp. 10–11.

21. Martingale, pp. 99–114.

22. Martina Helmerich, "Ein Wolf, der Blut trinkt," *Der Spiegel*, 1995, www.spiegel.de/spiegel/print/d-9183313.html.

23. Paula Vilella, "El 'Hannibal Lecter de los Andes,' 11 años en el limbo legal," *El Mundo*, 2010, http://www.elmundo.es/america/2010/01/20/noticias/1264016111.html.
24. Martingale, pp. 131–151.
25. "Serial Child Killer Tsutomu Miyazaki, 2 Others Executed," *Japan Today*, http://www.japantoday.com/category/crime/view/serial-child-killer-tsutomu-miyazaki-executed.
26. "Yoo Yeong Chul," crimeZZZ.net, http://www.crimezzz.net/serialkiller_news/Y/YOO_yeong_chul.php.
27. Robert Kalman, *Born to Kill in the USSR: True Stories of Soviet Serial Killers* (Victoria, BC, Canada: FriesenPress, 2014), pp. 293–301.

Chapter 4: Understanding Cannibalistic Serial Killers

1. Moira Martingale, *Cannibal Killers: The History of Impossible Murderers* (New York: St. Martin's Press, 1995), p. 186.
2. Hannah Scott, "The 'Gentler Sex': Patterns in Female Serial Murder," in Richard N. Kocsis, ed., *Serial Murder and the Psychology of Violent Crimes* (Totowa, NJ: Humana Press, 2008), p. 186.
3. Martingale, p. 50.
4. George B. Palermo, "Narcissism, Sadism, and Loneliness: The Case of Serial Killer Jeffrey Dahmer," in Richard N. Kocsis, ed., *Serial Murder and the Psychology of Violent Crimes* (Totowa, NJ: Humana Press, 2008), p. 86.
5. Robert J. Morton, ed., *Serial Murder: Multi-Disciplinary Perspectives for Investigators*, https://www.fbi.gov/stats-services/publications/serial-murder/serial-murder-july-2008-pdf, p. 14.
6. Berit Broograd, "The Making of a Serial Killer: Possible Social Causes of Psychopathology," *Psychology Today*, 2012, https://www.psychologytoday.com/blog/the-superhuman-mind/201212/the-making-serial-killer.

7. Petra Klages, *Serienmord und Kannibalismus in Deutschland: Fallstudien, Psychologie, Profiling* (Graz, Austria: V.F. Sammler, 2011), p. 207.
8. Karen Franklin, "Homicidal Triad: Predictor of Violence or Urban Myth?," *Psychology Today*, 2012, https://www.psychologytoday.com/blog/witness/201205/homicidal-triad-predictor-violence-or-urban-myth.
9. Morton, p. 2.

active cannibalism—Cannibalism that includes killing the victim first.

anthropophagy—Eating the flesh of human beings; synonym for cannibalism among humans.

autocannibalism—Also called self-cannibalism, this is the act of consuming parts of one's own body.

cannibalism—The act of consuming parts of a member of the same species.

degenerate—An immoral or corrupt person.

endocannibalism—Cannibalism committed on someone belonging to the same group as the cannibal.

exocannibalism—Cannibalism committed on someone not belonging to the same group as the cannibal.

medicinal cannibalism—Cannibalism committed in the belief that it will have a healing effect.

necrophagy—Eating carrion, the flesh of the dead.

paraphilia—Paraphilias or paraphilic disorders are atypical sexual interests that are either distressing for the person who has them or involve harm coming to another person.

passive cannibalism—An act of cannibalism where the cannibalized person is not killed for the purpose of eating them.

placentophagy—Consuming the placenta after the birth of a child.

psychopath—A person with antisocial personality disorder, the symptoms of which include callousness and a lack of empathy.

psychosis—A mental disorder that is characterized by losing contact with reality, for example, hearing voices that are not there.

quack—An untrained person who nonetheless dispenses medical treatment and advice.

serial killer—A person who kills at least two people in different events, which are separated by a cooling-off period.

vampirism—The act of drinking the blood of a member of the same species.

Further Reading

Books

Bonn, Scott. *Why We Love Serial Killers. The Curious Appeal of the World's Most Savage Killers.* New York: Skyhorse Publishing, 2014.

Davidson, Peter. *Death by Cannibal: Minds with an Appetite for Murder.* New York: Berkley Books, 2015.

Fox, James Alan and Levin, Jack. *Extreme Killing: Understanding Serial and Mass Murder.* Thousand Oaks, CA: SAGE Publications, 2015.

Haycock, Dean. *Murderous Minds: Exploring the Psychopathic Brain: Neurological Imaging and the Manifestation of Evil.* New York and London: Pegasus Books, 2014.

Kiehl, Kent A. *The Psychopath Whisperer: The Science of Those Without Conscience.* New York: Crown Publishers, 2014.

Wilson, David, Yardley, Elisabeth and Lynes, Adam. *Serial Killers and the Phenomenon of Serial Murder: A Student Textbook.* Sherfield on Loddon, England: Waterside Press, 2015.

Websites

National Museum of Crime & Punishment
www.crimemuseum.org/

The Crime Museum in Washington, DC, shows the American history of crime, law enforcement, and punishment.

The Serial Killer Database Research Project
skdb.fgcu.edu/info.asp

The Serial Killer Database Research Project collects data on serial killers and presents public statistics.

Movies

Alive. Directed by Frank Marshall, 1993.
The Silence of the Lambs. Directed by Jonathan Demme, 1991.

Index